MW01204321

We Fought Like Lions

We Fought Like Lions

A Polish Jewish Soldier's Odyssey

Through the Holocaust:

Warsaw Uprising to Nazi POW

Gary Lelonek, MD

DEDICATION

Two years have already gone by after the terrible events of the war. We, the survivors of Sierpc, in an effort to commemorate the town in which we were born and where we lived until Hitler wrought havoc, have decided to give a written account of all those events. Immediately after the war there was no possibility to have this book printed, because we did not yet know of each other and because we were not in a position to put down our thoughts. After life slowly resumed its normal path we formed a committee in charge of mutual assistance and of establishing permanent connection among the members. It is our aim to create a book on all those events that happened during the war.

This book is meant to be a monument commemorating all those beloved persons that died or were killed in action as heroes.

-The Editors.

Introduction from *Zaml Book Fun Sierpcer Shairit HaChurban.*[1] Published in 1948 by the Sierpcer Jewish Committee (US Zone Germany). Charlie Shayah Lelonek is listed as one of five people on the book's Coordinator Committee.

We Fought Like Lions is dedicated to the memory of Charlie Shayah Lelonek, Yeshayahu ben Yitzchak Mayer and all the victims and survivors of Sierpc, Poland. May their neshamahot[2] have many aliyot.[3]

---

[1] The Complete Book of the Sierpcer People Left Over From the Destruction.

[2] Souls.

[3] Spiritual elevations of the soul in the world to come.

We are here among the singular families that were by some miracle saved from the heavy folk tragedy. It is not so simple or obvious to maintain a family whole. One can't perhaps write out, and I hope that when I have the opportunity when I am together with you in America, will we be able to discuss and clarify things which are not until today still not clear. I, myself, Shayah Lelonek, have endured a history of suffering and pain on the battlefield until the German captivity in camps. Fate wanted me to remain alive and be able to tell all in freedom. Maybe there are already with you Sierpcer people who came after the war and they will explain to you, more or less, a chapter of Jewish life in the years 1939-1945.

-Charlie Shayah Lelonek
May 16, 1947
Lampertheim displaced persons camp

CONTENTS

Charlie Shayah Lelonek aka Stanislaw Jelonek in the Polish People's Army uniform. Charlie was known as Charles, Shayah, Szaja, Yeshayah, Yeshayahu and Stanislaw.

Rose Rakow
b: 1844
bp: Biezun, Plock, Russia

Israel (Shaya AzIel) Kadetsky
b: 1845
bp: Biezun, Plock, Russia
d: Dec 20, 1900
dp: Biezun, Plock, Russia

Pesia Bajla Kadecki
b: Apr 14, 1887
bp: Biezun, Plock, Russia
d: Jun 24, 1967
dp: Chaifa, Israel

Matla (Miriam) Pilnikiewcz
bp: Sierpc, Poland

Abram (Avraham Hersch) Lelonek
b: 1834
bp: Sierpc, Poland

Icek Majer (Yizchak Mayer) Lelonek
b: Oct 5, 1884
bp: Sierpc, Poland
d: May 31, 1967
dp: Chaifa, Israel

Tzvi Hersch Lelonek
b: Feb 19, 1925
bp: Sierpc, Poland

Tova Lelonek
bp: Sierpc, Poland

Moshe Rueven Lelonek
b: Feb 1, 1922
bp: Sierpc, Poland
d: Nov 24, 2009
dp: Chaifa, Israel

Miriam (Mleta) Lelonek
b: Dec 22, 1919
bp: Sierpc, Poland

Chaim Lelonek
b: Jun 17, 1917
bp: Sierpc, Poland
d: ? 1940

Charlie (Yeshaya) Lelonek
b: Jun 12, 1914
bp: Sierpc, Poland
d: Sep 16, 1994
dp: Brooklyn, Kings, New York

Bluma Lelonek
b: Mar 1912
bp: Sierpc, Poland
d: Aug 26, 2011
dp: Chaifa, Israel

Charlie (Yeshaya) Lelonek & Sylvia Haskel

Joel Lelonek

Cliff Lelonek

Robin Lelonek

Michael Lelonek

Steven Lelonek

David Lelonek

Richard Lelonek

ACKNOWLEDGMENTS

I have been fortunate to work with many people while researching my grandfather, Charlie Szaja Lelonek's, memoir. My uncle, David Lelonek, conducted the interview of his father in 1980 and answered many questions about Charlie and the interview. The Museum of Jewish Heritage - A Living Memorial to the Holocaust, preserved the interview and sent me a copy. The YIVO Institute (Yiddish Scientific Institute) for Jewish Research scanned and sent me a copy of the Yizkor book[4] that Charlie worked on, *Zaml Book Fun Sierpcer Shairit HaChurban*. Charlie grew up in Sierpc, Poland and memorialized his community in the book. The YIVO Institute also allowed me to photograph the thirty-three letters that the family wrote to the Sierpcer Relief Committee in New York during their time in the Lampertheim displaced persons camp. The United States Holocaust Memorial Museum (USHMM) shared the International Tracing Service (ITS) archive records[5] of the Lelonek family's refugee experience after the war and the process of immigrating to Israel and America. Sylvia Lelonek, Charlie's wife and my grandmother, and I discussed Charlie's leadership, dedication to his family and his strong will and character. She shared Charlie's photo album from the Lampertheim displaced persons camp, which includes family pictures in the displaced persons

---

[4] Memorial books were written by survivors to preserve the memory of their towns and the people murdered in the Holocaust.
[5] To search the ITS archives you can visit the USHMM website and search for ITS or use the following link: http://itsrequest.ushmm.org/its/contact_form.php

camp, various ID photos of him, a photo of him in his Polish People's Army uniform and photos of murdered cousins.

Thank you to the volunteers at JewishGen and Jewish Records Indexing-Poland.[6] Through the JewishGen Family Finder (JGFF),[7] I was able to connect with both Kadetsky, the Americanized version of the original polish Kadecki surname, (Charlie's mother's family) and Lelonek researchers to reconnect and reconstruct both family trees. *Kehilat Sierpc; Sefer Zikaron,*[8] published in Tel Aviv in 1959, is the expanded second edition of the Yizkor book Charlie Lelonek had worked on. It has been translated by JewishGen. The book has information about the lives of the Lelonek and Kadetsky families in Sierpc, Poland and a list of family members who were murdered during the Holocaust.[9] The vital records and letters of the Lelonek family were translated by volunteers through JewishGen's Viewmate service. JewishGen's mission is to "encourage the preservation of Jewish heritage, allowing anyone with Jewish ancestry to research their roots, connect with relatives, and learn about their family history." Mission accomplished!

I owe a tremendous amount of gratitude to my family. My in-laws, Rene and June Slotkin, have been supportive of my family in too many ways to list. A survivor himself, Rene and I have discussed the Holocaust and the importance of sharing and preserving the events and accounts of Holocaust survivors. My father, Joel, and I discussed his father's philosophy, perspective on G-d as well as his wartime experiences. I could always count on my father's encouragement to

---

6 To search Polish vital records visit the JRI Poland with the following link: http://jri-poland.org/jriplweb.htm You will need to use the town's geographic coordinates, Sierpc is 5253 1940, Biezun is 5258 1955. For other towns coordinates use the "your town" tab.

7 To search and list entries in the JewishGen Family Finder database use the following link: http://www.jewishgen.org/jgff/ You will need to create a free account to search the database.

8 Community of Sierpc Memorial Book.

9 www.jewishgen.org/yizkor/Sierpc/Sierpc.html

keep digging when my research hit a dead-end, or when life took me in other directions. He proofread my research and advised me on self-publishing. My mother, Karen, read and edited my work and discussed Charlie's perspective on orthodox Judaism. My sisters, Judith Arnall and Cheryl Jacob, and I shared our memories of Grandpa Charlie. We realized that we had inherited many of Charlie's character traits that enabled him to save his family and to be a soldier. My brother-in-law, Rabbi Daniel Arnall of blessed memory, got me started on genealogy in 1999. He and my sister Cheryl's husband, Yaacov Jacob, always wanted to hear the latest in my research. My children, Chaya Sarah, Yehuda, and Penina are my inspiration for preserving this history. Our family's history enriches our lives. My wife, Mia, has always encouraged me to continue the research and spend the time I needed to invest in the project. She is unwavering in her love and support. She offered her considerable talents in designing the book's cover. Finally, I thank G-d, for supporting my grandfather through the war. My brother-in-law, Yaacov Jacob, once remarked after a discovery, "This is incredible Gary!!! I can't believe you continue to find such gems. I guess it's just as the rabbis say, "In the way a man wants to go, G-d will help him." (Talmud tractate Makkos page 10b) It seemed that the more effort and time that I spent researching, the more Charlie's experiences were revealed to me by G-d.

PREFACE

The enormity of the Holocaust is impossible to comprehend. Growing up with two grandfathers who were survivors, the subject was always close to the surface and yet suppressed. My grandfathers did not discuss what they had gone through during World War II, yet with Holocaust remembrance days and Holocaust education, a heightened awareness and sensitivity to the Holocaust was part of my childhood.

Attending Yavneh Academy elementary school in Paramus NJ, eighth grade was spent studying the Holocaust with Mrs. Gabriella Weiss, herself a survivor. Every year the eighth graders write and produce a play based on our studies. When we visited the United States Holocaust Memorial Museum in Washington, DC I was unable to fathom what the murder of six million people meant. The attack on the United States of America on September 11, 2001 with the loss of 2,977 innocent lives, put the toll of the Holocaust into perspective. That day that I realized the death and emotional toll of September 11, would have to continue for 2,015 consecutive days (five and a half years), to reach the magnitude of the 6,000,000 Jews murdered by the Nazis during the Holocaust.

As a husband and father, my feelings and understanding about Holocaust grows. Every year on Tishah B'Av, the 9th of the Jewish month of Av, I cry and mourn the murder of my family members in the Holocaust. Throughout Jewish history, Tishah B'Av has been designated as the day to mourn, the loss of the two Temples in Jerusalem and tragedies that have befallen the Jewish community throughout history. Instead of viewing each calamity as an isolated event, they are connected through Tishah B'Av, as an opportunity to examine the community's actions, relationship with G-d and to collectively petition G-d to stop punishing the Jewish people. The Jewish community spends the day mourning together in synagogue, engages in a communal fast, sits on the floor and reads dirges of communal calamities. Holocaust dirges have been added to the Tishah B'Av service. I sit and fast with my community remembering the Holocaust, honoring the memory of those who were murdered as well as the ongoing wound of the survivors.

We Fought Like Lions is the testimony of my grandfather's, Charlie Shayah Lelonek, experiences during World War II. Although his formal name was Charles, he was known to everyone as Charlie and to his grandchildren as "Grandpa Charlie." His narrative is important to share because it is an example of how Jews fought and actively sought to protect themselves and others. The story combats many stereotypes of the Jews in the Holocaust. Charlie was able to blend in with the indigenous populations while maintaining his identity and pride as a Pole and a Jew. He was acutely aware of the political dangers surrounding him. At the outset of the war, he recognized the potential life threatening danger that the Nazi political platform of anti-Semitism carried. Inaction was not an option. Survival was hanging in the balance. Divine providence, his vision of the time and his strength of character enabled him to save his parents and siblings from the destruction of the Nazis. In September 1939, he debated with and convinced his father to move the family to the Soviet Union. While this posed an existential threat to their Jewish identity, remaining in German-occupied Poland held a death sentence. Charlie literally carried his mother on his back to the Russian frontier. When Charlie enlisted in the Polish division of the Russian Army, his family was treated as Russian citizens instead of Polish refugees and was thereby entitled to better resettlement and rations. He enlisted in the army with the ideal of liberating Poland so it could be a free democratic country. He believed that fighting and destroying the evil of the Nazis was worth the risk of his own life. After the war, Charlie addressed the threat of communism to Judaism and facilitated his family's emigration from Russia to join him in the US zone in Germany.

During my research, I glimpsed the ordeal my grandfather lived through. Although Charlie and his immediate family escaped the fate of the concentration camps, they lived in fear for their lives, were exiled and on the run as refugees for ten years. They lost Charlie's brother, Chaim Lelonek, as well as over 32 cousins, aunts, and uncles murdered by Nazis. They witnessed the leaders of their town, Sierpc, and Jews from their area being dehumanized, demoralized, tortured and murdered. I cried as I listened to the emotion in my grandfather's voice during the taped interview, where he expresses his grief and his anger. He channeled his emotions into the drive to fight the Nazis and survive.

The Lelonek family's letters to the Sierpc Relief Committee after the war, capture the emotional sentiment of survivors. While my grandfather's interview was conducted 30-40 years after the events he lived through, the letters are the family's real-time account of their experience. They possess an immediacy and authenticity that might otherwise be questioned regarding my grandfather's interview recorded decades later, shaped by memory, time and perspective. The family wrote 33 letters from 1946-1949, describing life in the Lampertheim displaced persons camp, the Holocaust, the establishment of the State of Israel and the emotional toll the uncertainty of where they will live and when they will be able to continue their lives. On March 16, 1947, Charlie wrote about the sadness for the murder of family and friends:

> The tears are stuck in one's throat, the heart breaks
> from hurt, reading the names of our most loved, dear,

and closest holy ones, kedoshim,[10] who have perished in such a beastly manner at the hands of Hitler's bandits. We bow our heads to the fallen and murdered - our sisters and brothers!!! To eternal memory!

The tone of some of the letters is contemptuous and enraged that the world had forgotten the refugees and moved on with their lives while the refugees languished with no idea when their exile would end. On December 17, 1946, Bluma Lazinsky wrote:

> Today I received a little a little piece of paper from you, in which you write, that you haven't understood my first letter. Yes, it is true, I, actually, do believe, that you are not able to understand such letters, because people, who live in good conditions, cannot realize and don't want to understand, how life in the camp is, without a home, without means to live and so on… You all, who present the Sierpcer Relief Committee, what do you understand? To respond to long, painful letters with small, cold two words! And therefore, the question read: What have all of you achieved, already? Whom did you give a help, already? There isn't more than dry and cold relationship to be seen from you! That it is, on paper you're declaiming as a Sierpcer Relief Committee - well, that's true - paper is patient! You can write, what you want. And it is: The rich one does not believe the hungry one and I won't write more about this because my heart feels too much hurt. Well, anyway, I believe, that you, possibly, will understand this letter, and with a good will, you actually, will understand… I close my letter with greetings to the Sierpcer Relief Committee and to you and family.

On July 22, 1947, Bluma Lazinsky shared her thoughts and

---

10 Lit. Holy ones. Used in reference to people who died in the name of G-d.

emotions about the establishment of the State of Israel after the murder of 6 million Jews:[11]

> I am happy to have lived to see the day we have our own country. It is only very, very sad that our 6 million martyrs didn't live to have the joy to see this day. Because of that, my joy is clouded; many of my nearest and dearest dreamed and fought for this moment and didn't live to see it, although they longed so much for this land and so much blood has been spilled for it. Now I hope to be able to reconstruct my life there and build a future.

After surviving the Holocaust, Charlie Lelonek was angry at G-d, the Nazis, and the Polish people. When he arrived in America, survivors were urged not to dwell on the past but to start anew. After the initial shock of the Holocaust, the world consciously tried to put the war behind them and concentrate on reconstruction. In Israel, his siblings were met with disapprobation for their tardy Zionism[12] and for allegedly have gone "as lambs to the slaughter house." It was easier to repress the traumatic memories than to risk being misunderstood or disbelieved. Charlie's wife, Sylvia Lelonek, said that once they started

---

[11] In November 1945, Dr. Wilhelm Hoettl, an Austrian-born official in the Third Reich and a trained historian who served in a number of senior positions in the SS, testified for the prosecution in the Nuremberg trials of accused Nazi war criminals as well as the Adolf Eichmann trial in 1961. He described a conversation he had with Eichmann, the SS official whose principal responsibility was for the logistics of the Jewish genocide, in Budapest in August 1944. In the 1961 testimony, Hoettl recalled how "Eichmann … told me that, according to his information, some 6,000,000 Jews had perished until then- 4,000,000 in extermination camps and the remaining 2,000,000 through shooting by the Operations Units and other causes, such as disease, etc." The Nuremberg trials were well covered by the media and followed anxiously by survivors in the displaced persons camps. More than 400 visitors observed the proceedings every day for a year, in addition to 325 newspaper, radio, and newsreel correspondents from 23 different countries.

[12] The philosophical desire of the Jewish people to return to the Land of Israel.

talking about having children, Charlie shared that he really wanted to have a large family. He saw this as a continuation of the fight against Hitler and the Nazi's agenda to wipe out the Jews. With Sylvia, Charlie managed to reestablish himself and restart his life. When Charlie recorded his wartime account in 1980, he was 66 years old, had 7 children and 7 grandchildren, with another grandchild on the way. He had already experienced the natural deaths of his parents in Israel and seen his siblings rebuild their lives and start families in Israel. Developmental psychologist Erik Erikson describes that at this stage of life, people pass through the psychosocial crisis of ego integrity versus despair. We contemplate our accomplishments and are able to develop integrity if we see ourselves as leading a successful life. Success in this stage will lead to the virtue of wisdom. Wisdom enables a person to look back on their life with a sense of closure and completeness, and also accept death without fear. Charlie studied the Holocaust and reconciled his anger, viewing his ordeal through a personal and historical perspective. He was ready to delve back into his past and pass it on to his family. Research has demonstrated that sharing of the family's past, both positive and negative stories, functions to support and build resilience for future generations. Children who know their family history, who have shared in these stories, develop a sense of self embedded in a larger familial and intergenerational context, and this sense of self provides strength and security.[13] [14]

As I researched the account, I felt a special connection to my grandfather. He believed in remembering and preserving the history of his town and family. He believed his actions made a difference. In publishing my grandfather's testimony, I feel I am continuing that effort as well as participating in the resistance. To me, "never again"

---

[13] Duke, M., Lazarus, A., & Fivush, R. "Knowledge of Family History as a Clinically Useful Index of Psychological Well-Being and Prognosis: A Brief Report." Psychotherapy: Theory, Research, Practice, Training, Vol 45(2), Jun 2008, 268-272.
[14] Fivush, R., Bohanek, J.G., & Duke, M. "The Intergenerational Self: Subjective Perspective and Family History." In F. Sani (Ed.). Individual and Collective Self-Continuity. Mahwah, NJ: Erlbaum. 2008, 131-143.

means transmitting this philosophy of being proactive and knowing that the actions of one individual can make a difference.

While recalling his experiences, Charlie talks about Yom Kippur[15] twice; the first Yom Kippur of the war in 1939 and last Yom Kippur of the war in 1944. He discusses the beginning of the oppression by Nazis in 1939, when they denigrated the religious leaders of his town, Sierpc, on Yom Kippur. Later, he speaks about how he fought the Nazis in the Warsaw Uprising, going into battle on Rosh HaShanah,[16] September 16, 1944, and continuing to fight ten days later on Yom Kippur. In the aftermath of the quelling of the Warsaw Uprising, Charlie was captured by the Nazis. The Russian Army informed Charlie's parents that he was "missing in action" and he was declared dead. His family sat shivah[17] and said Kaddish[18] for him. Incredibly, fifty years later to the day, after Yom Kippur came to a close on September 16, 1994, Charlie died.

As the high holidays started in 1994, Charlie was dying from cancer. On Rosh HaShanah, he insisted on being brought to the synagogue to hear the blowing of the shofar.[19] On Yom Kippur, he was too sick to go to synagogue. During Yom Kippur, he told his sons, Steven and David, that the angels were there for him but he would not leave without saying goodbye to his wife Sylvia who was in the synagogue. When Sylvia returned home, Charlie told her that the angels were there to take him. Sylvia told him that it was okay to go, they said goodbye and he died.

Yom Kippur describes how Charlie was judged. Charlie's time to die did not come in the beginning of the Nazi occupation of Poland in

---

[15] Day of atonement spent fasting and praying in the synagogue after reflecting and repenting.

[16] Holiday celebrating Jewish New Year.

[17] Jewish mourning period for seven days after the burial of the deceased.

[18] Memorial prayer.

[19] Ram's horn fashioned into a wind instrument, sounded one hundred times each of the two days of Rosh HaShanah.

1939, nor was it his time at the Warsaw Uprising in 1944. During the war Charlie had survived all the situations of death listed in the Yom Kippur liturgy; "who will live, who will die, who in his intended time, who not in his intended time." He was victimized by Nazi machine gun fire strafing his squadron and the drowning of his comrades as they crossed the Vistula river into a burning Warsaw. He knew the hunger and thirst of the POWs, the punishing weather of Siberia and the sickness on the battlefields. He had wounds from frostbite and shrapnel. He endured being stripped of everything and seeing the survivors with their spirits broken. For the rest of his life, he endured nightmares of the Nazis chasing and capturing him. Time and again he states, "I survived that too." He lived another fifty years until his intended time; until his final judgment on Yom Kippur 1994.

Every Yom Kippur, I think about my grandfather. I know he was chosen to survive and through his grandchildren and great-grandchildren he continues to live. As Yom Kippur closes we say "Adonoy, hu haElohim"[20] seven times. The rabbis teach that we say this phrase to accompany G-d, whose presence has been so palpable during the time from Rosh HaShanah to Yom Kippur, back through the seven mystical levels of the world. I know that I am accompanying my grandfather's soul as well.

Charlie was named after the prophet Yeshayah, Isaiah. Isaiah is a Jewish prophet who lived during the time of the destruction of the Northern Jewish Kingdom and the exile of the ten tribes. He had prophetic visions of the destruction and exile of the people as well as the return of the people, their repentance and rebuilding of Jerusalem. His prophecies are a source of comfort as they discuss hope for the future of the Jewish people. The book of Isaiah is both the source of

---

[20] Lit. "The Master, only He is G-d." This the last line of the ending prayer of Yom Kippur, the Neilah (closing) Service. The Jewish people at the end of the service declare G-d's sovereignty seven times. The seven pronunciations symbolize the seven levels of heaven through which God ascends and returns after the Yom Kippur service.

the destructive "Vision of Isaiah" read on the Sabbath before Tishah B'Av, and the seven prophecies of consolation that are read for the seven weeks following Tishah B'Av until Rosh HaShanah, a time of renewal. Charlie survived the destruction of the Holocaust, and his vision of the times, enabled his family to survive, return to Israel and rebuild their lives. He witnessed the establishment of the State of Israel and lived to see his children, grandchildren, siblings, nieces and nephews thrive.

I have purposefully left a mistake in the text, so let me know if you find it ☺.

Gary Lelonek
wefoughtlikelions@gmail.com
Charlie Shayah Lelonek's grandson
June 16, 2016

INTRODUCTION

Charlie Lelonek was a great storyteller. His son, David, under the direction of professor Yaffa Eliach, gave Charlie the opportunity to provide his testimony. Charlie opens the interview talking about his hometown and the Lelonek family's history and continues on his train of thought through the family's resettlement in 1949. David's interviewing technique allowed Charlie to lead the interview with few directed questions. Even when David did use questions to direct the interview, Charlie would preface his answer with background information to put the question in context. David opens the beginning of the second recording session with a question about the family's situation while Charlie was a prisoner of war. Charlie responds to the question, "Not exactly…. I will start a little earlier." Charlie was interested in responding to David's question, framing his answer in the proper context. He, therefore, starts his answer from an earlier point. He addressed the question by explaining the impact of his enlistment in the Russian division of the Polish People's Army on the lives of his family. He then continues with the family's reality while he was a prisoner of war.

Rather than using the interview to write Charlie's memoir in my voice, I chose to maintain the integrity of Charlie's voice by transcribing the interview verbatim. I have translated Yiddish, Hebrew or German words in the footnotes and the glossary. When I inserted information into the text of his interview, italics are employed to clearly allow the eye to distinguish the insertion from the interview. Charlie traveled extensively through Europe and the Soviet Union. I have identified many of the cities that he mentions. I have included travel distances from city to city to help the reader conceptualize the magnitude of his journeys.

The interview spans seven recording sessions. The first two sessions form the bulk of the interview, in which Charlie shares his journey. In the next five recording sessions, David follows up with more directed questions about Charlie's experiences. For organizational clarity, I have divided the book into parts and chapters. Part I provides background information to the interview and Part II is David's interview of Charlie. I have included my sources, the Lelonek family's letters while living in the displaced persons camp, the testimonies of two of Charlie's siblings and inserts with historical background information. The supplemental material verifies and frames the narrative. The reader will be able to place events within the wider historical context.

Charlie's account was carefully researched and verified. The interview was conducted thirty-five years after the end of World War II and spans the events during the years of 1939-1949. Using the primary resources, I have independently verified many aspects of the interview and identified potential inaccuracies. For instance, Charlie recounts fighting in the Warsaw Uprising in September 1943, while it is well-known that the Warsaw Uprising occurred in August to October 1944. Russian military records verify that Charlie fought in September 1944 in the Warsaw Uprising and was declared missing in action. I have left inaccuracies unchanged and use parenthesizes, with accurate information, as well as footnotes stating my sources.

Another resource used to establish the veracity of the Charlie's account are the letters that the Lelonek family wrote immediately after the war, which are included in Part V of *We Fought Like Lions*. The letters, written from 1946-1948, are fresh descriptions of their reality during the war and in the displaced persons camps. The letters possess an immediacy and authenticity that might otherwise be questioned in the interview, as it was conducted thirty-five years after the war. The consistency of the accounts of the interview and the letters adds authenticity and validity to the interview.

The individual narratives of Charlie, his sister Bluma Lazinsky (Part III) and brother, Moshe Lelonek (Part IV), together offer a multidimensional perspective of one family's reality. They were written independently of each other, in different years and with different agendas. Charlie was being interviewed to document his testimony as a matter of a historical record. Bluma was requesting reparations for her hand injury. Moshe was sharing with his great-grandchildren in order to pass on the family history. Charlie's motivation led him to describe his experiences in detail. Bluma focused directly on establishing that her hand was injured during the time and circumstances that qualified her for reparations from Germany. Moshe focused on the journey that led him from Poland to Israel. Viewed together, their statements corroborate each other, adding a depth and validity greater than the individual accounts on their own.

To generalize Charlie's testimony, I have included "historical context" inserts. These inserts serve to the demonstrate the effects of the political decisions and global events on the Lelonek family. The "historical contexts" were reprinted with permission from Encyclopedia Britannica, Yad Vashem and the United States Holocaust Memorial Museum.

Charlie's interview you can be heard or downloaded it at;

http://tinyurl.com/charlielelonek

PART I

INTRODUCTION TO CHARLIE LELONEK'S TESTIMONY

CHAPTER 1

DIGGING FOR TREASURE

"Getty."

I am a "Sukkot[21] baby." I was born during the Jewish holiday of Sukkot in October. Every year, Grandpa Charlie, Mama Sylvia and uncles David, Steven and Richard and his fiancé Stacey came to have dinner and birthday cake in the sukkah.[22] We also celebrated Mama Sylvia's and my younger sister Cheryl's birthdays, since we all have birthdays in October. Mama Sylvia always brought Entenmanns Louisiana Crunch cake (which I love but it is dairy) and my mom made my favorite dinner, "hotdog thing," known to everyone else as calypso franks and beans. (Which meant no dairy Louisiana Crunch cake after this meat meal since my parents and grandparents observed the kosher[23] laws. I would enjoy the cake another day.) We ate outside in the sukkah, wearing our winter jackets. My big sister Judith, baked and decorated a cake. Celebrating all the birthdays together made Sukkot

---

[21] The holiday commemorating the ways Jews lived after the Exodus from Egypt, in huts for forty years in the desert before entering the Land of Israel.

[22] The huts that Jews dwell in during the holiday of Sukkot. The sukkahs commemorate the way the Jews lived in the desert after the Exodus from Egypt and symbolize that people are reliant on G-d's beneficence.

[23] Jewish dietary laws.

the most festive part of the year. I loved spending the time with my grandparents and knew that the feeling was mutual.

Grandpa Charlie always engaged Judith, Cheryl and me in conversation about our Jewish or secular studies and he was interested in our opinions. Judith, Cheryl and I attended modern orthodox day schools. We saw Charlie for the last time before Yom Kippur 1994 when Judith was 18, Cheryl was 8 and I was 14. He was battling cancer, weak and tired. He asked Judith about a kashrut related practice and was interested in her opinion. He very much enjoyed these conversations. He pronounced our names with a polish accent. Mine was pronounced as "Getty." I thought it was interesting to be referred to like the gasoline company. It was a loving sound to hear my name pronounced that way. I never asked him about his World War II experiences and he never volunteered to speak to me about them. By the time I was interested to know his account, he had passed away.

In 2000, I started researching my family history. Shortly after my big sister Judith married Daniel Arnall, Daniel asked me to help him with a project in his office. It was March 2000, and I was studying for the year in Israel. I flew into LA for Passover[24] to surprise my parents who thought I was staying in Israel for the holiday. Daniel and I hung out in his office, which was fun since Daniel stocked his office with all sorts of candies. In addition to managing real estate, Daniel thought he owned a candy shop, as his office pantry and a desk drawer were overflowing with Hershey's chocolate. Daniel was working on his family tree and he asked me to tell him about my family. I had never researched the family tree before and I was only able to name primary relatives. After Passover, I returned to Israel having decided to interview my grandfather's siblings who were all living in Israel. I was privileged to interview Charlie's oldest sister, Bluma Lazinsky who had just turned 89. It was interesting to interview her. I had visited her earlier in the year, with an Israeli cousin, without the agenda of mining

---

[24] Holiday celebrating emancipation and the Exodus from Egypt.

for the family history. Now I returned on my own to speak with her. I was a bit of a novelty to my Israeli family. I had never been to Israel before studying for the academic year of 1999-2000. Though my uncles had visited Israel before me, I was the first American-born relative who was able to converse with my grandfather's siblings in Hebrew. They spoke Yiddish, Hebrew, and Polish but not English. I had learned Hebrew and studied Jewish texts in school, and was comfortable although not fluent in the language. Conducting an interview in Hebrew was a challenge and Bluma weathered the interview. She had not been in contact with some relatives since she was a child and she was unable to remember many names. She fondly recalled hearing the Purim[25] scroll read in her grandparent's house in Sierpc. She told me that Charlie's mother, Pesa Lelonek nee Kadetsky, had brothers William, Abraham, Cheskel, Moshe, and a sister Rachel Wolman. No one knew what had happened to them. I had hit a dead-end.

For 8 years I was unable to uncover any traces of the Kadetsky family. Then, in 2009, I connected with another Kadetsky researcher, Mark Hallerman, through JewishGen's Family Finder. I saw that he was researching the Kadetsky family from the same town as I was. We each only had segments of the tree and only through Bluma Lazinsky's recollection of Rachel Wolman did we realize that we were related. We collaborated and figured out that our grandfathers, Charlie Lelonek and Abraham Wolman, were first cousins, making us third cousins. Analyzing Ellis Island ship manifests[26] and Polish vital records, I traced the Kadecki family back to the 1760's in Biezun, Poland. I found Bluma Lazinsky's and Charlie Lelonek's "Pages of Testimony" on the Yad Vashem "Central Database for Shoah Victims' Names"[27] that recorded the Kadetsky and Lelonek cousins, aunts, and uncles who were murdered in the Holocaust. Charlie's mother, Pesa, was the

---

[25] Holiday commemorate the story of Esther.

[26] To search the Ellis Island use the following link: http://ellisisland.org/

[27] To search the Yad Vashem Central Database for Shoah Victims' Names on online you can visit the Yad Vashem website or use the following link: http://db.yadvashem.org/names/search.html?language=en

youngest of nine children, and six of her older siblings had come to America from 1890-1920. I even discovered my grandfather's middle name. I shared with my uncle Richard that Charlie's grandfather was named Szaja Zeile Kadecki. He then told me that in the early 1990s he and his brother were once watching a NY Mets versus the St. Louis Cardinals baseball game on TV and the play caller announced that the next Cardinals' batter up to bat was Todd Zeile. Charlie happened to be sitting on the couch and told his sons: "Hey, that's my name." They were bewildered as he had never shared that before. That story made more sense to Richard now that I shared with him that Charlie's grandfather's name was Shayah Zeile Kadecki. Mark Hallerman connected me with another relative, Beth McGreen, the granddaughter of Charlie's uncle William Kadetsky. In December 2009, I contacted Beth for the first time. I shared with her the research on the tree. She responded "I do remember some cousins coming over from Europe and staying in the Bronx apartment. My family lived in the same building. I even remember being a flower girl when I was 3 at the man's wedding." I sent her pictures of my grandparent's wedding and she identified her grandparents under the wedding canopy along with herself as the flower girl.

After learning that William Kadetsky hosted my grandfather, I realized that I did not know much about my grandfather's life before coming to America. In January 2010, I sent an email out to my uncles to asking, "How did Grandpa Charlie get to America?" My uncle David Lelonek shared with me that Charlie had come from a displaced persons camp, immigrated to America and stayed with his uncle William Kadetsky. I was encouraged to find that information matched well to my research.

In August 2010, I sent an inquiry to the United States Holocaust Memorial Museum (USHMM) to search the International Tracing Service (ITS) archive for information about Chaim Lelonek, Charlie's brother, who had disappeared after being arrested by the Russians while the family was fleeing the Nazis in 1940. The ITS archive was established by the Allied powers after World War II to help reunite families separated during the war and to trace missing family members. The ITS has millions of pages of documentation that the Allies confiscated during the war. On May 24, 2012, almost two years after my inquiry, the USHMM sent me 36 documents from the ITS archive. They did not send any information about Chaim. His fate remains a mystery. Instead, all the documents pertained to Charlie, his parents and siblings!

The documents shed light on the Lelonek family's postwar journey from the Lampertheim displaced persons camp to America and Israel. Although the documents contained a timeline of their wartime locations, they lacked information about their experiences during the war. Upon sharing these documents with my uncles, my uncle Michael Lelonek, wrote on May 25, 2012, that "My brother David sat down with our father for about two weeks in 1981, as I recall, and he recorded and wrote down our father's story, in my father's own words."

With Charlie's the 18th yahrzeit,[28] approaching in September 2012, I emailed David about the recording. He responded; "I interviewed my dad for a Brooklyn College class I took about the Shoah." He told me that he had sent a copy to a Holocaust museum, but he did not recall which one. That day, I googled "Charlie Lelonek Holocaust." The top hit is a holding at the Museum of Jewish Heritage in Manhattan for "Testimony of Charlie Lelonek." I contacted the curator of their collection, Esther Brumberg, and she sent me a copy of the interview. I had hoped that I would receive the interview by Charlie's yahrzeit, the day after Yom Kippur, but it did not arrive in time. Sukkot that year began on October 1 and my family went away for the first two days. When we arrived home, I found an envelope from the Museum of Jewish Heritage had arrived.

I ripped the envelope open and found two CDs. I was ecstatic when

---

[28] Death anniversary according the Jewish lunar calendar.

I realized that there were two hours of audio recordings of Charlie's testimony. Thirty-two years after the interview had been recorded, it was back! I ran down the stairs with dinner to the sukkah in the backyard of my apartment building and listened to my grandfather join me in the sukkah one more time. I heard his Polish-accented voice for the first time since his death, 18 years earlier. He started "I was born in Poland. The name of the town is Sierpc…." Suddenly memories of Sukkot and birthdays past rushed into my consciousness and I heard him say to me again…"Getty."

CHAPTER 2

INTERVIEWING MY FATHER
BY DAVID LELONEK

Growing up, my siblings, five brothers, and one sister, knew that our father, Charlie Lelonek, had survived World War II and the Holocaust. He rarely spoke about it, only discussing it superficially, usually when he was reminded of those times by an incident or a person. Sadly, many of the stories ended with the referenced person passing away in the Shoah. Seeing the pain this recollection caused him, we rarely asked him questions about his war years.

In 1980, while attending Brooklyn College, I took a "Literature of the Holocaust" course, taught by professor Yaffa Eliach. Professor Eliach was a wonderful and kind person, a Holocaust survivor herself from Lithuania. An assignment for the course was to conduct a tape-recorded interview of our parents, grandparents or other close relatives who were Holocaust survivors. She pointed out that each survivor had a unique and special account to tell. As their numbers were dwindling, it was our obligation to try to document as many of them as possible. She understood that some survivors would not want to take part in these interviews, as it can be so painful for some to recall these events. For those who did not have access to a survivor, she had some survivors who volunteered to help with this project. To assist with our interviews, she developed guidelines to make the process a bit smoother. These interviews were done in conjunction with the Museum of Jewish Heritage - A Living Memorial to the Holocaust and they would eventually store copies of these tapes.

I obviously immediately thought that my father would be the right person for me to interview but I also knew the suffering it may cause him to recall these painful events. When I got home from college that day, I asked my mom, Sylvia Lelonek, if she felt if my dad would be willing to do the interviews. We discussed this idea for some time, concluding that the only way to really know was to ask him.

That evening, after my father came home from work and ate dinner, I quietly told him about the interview project which I had received that day. He listened to the instructions, read the questions and he told me he would have to think about it. Understanding how painful this could be for my father, I told him to take his time and I thanked him for considering it. The next morning, as my father and I had breakfast together, as we often did, he told me that he would do the interview. He said that we could do it in his bedroom, most likely needing a few nights to get through all the material. My dad expressed that it was indeed painful for him to speak about such things but he also knew that if he did not get his experiences from that time period on paper, that his testimony would be lost forever. I let him know how much I appreciated this opportunity to share this part of him with me.

That same evening, my father and I sat down together in his bedroom, closed the door, and asked all other family members to give us time to conduct this special interview. Over the next few nights, my father and I had the chance to share a once in a lifetime opportunity. Although there were times during the interview that seemed to be rather painful for my father, I thought my dad was very open and honest. He had excellent recall of many events. It was a wonderful bonding opportunity for me, spending this special time with my dad, making sure to respect these sacred stories. Through this interview, I heard many facts and stories about our family history for the first time in my life. My dad seemed pleased with the project as well, as he had the chance to tell his account, something the family could now hold on to and better understand these important events that helped form the man that he was.

Once the sessions were done, I put the interview to paper. The interviews gave me a new respect for my dad. I knew that he had been through a lot during the war, but the interviews helped me realize that my father had been through so much more than I could ever have imagined. In addition, by way of this project, my dad and I formed an even closer bond, which we shared until his passing in 1994.

About three years ago, my nephew Gary Lelonek, had asked about these interviews. Gary had become the de facto family genealogist, and he was researching information about my father and his war experiences. My brother, Michael Lelonek, mentioned to Gary that I had conducted these interviews while I was at Brooklyn College. Gary then asked me about the interviews, and the facts surrounding them. I knew that I had kept copies of them, but I was not exactly sure where they were. In time, I did find them but sadly the sound quality was terrible after over thirty years of just sitting in an envelope in my desk drawer. I felt awful. Thankfully Gary followed up with the Museum of Jewish Heritage, and they did find digital copies of my interview with my father. Gary was kind enough to immediately send me copies of those interviews. That evening I listened to all of them. I was brought back to 1980 and those interviews. It was so emotional and touching for me to listen to my father once again. Hearing my father's voice, a flood of emotions came over me. As I listened to his voice, hearing his unique intonations and expressions, I could not help but shed a few tears, wishing that he were still here with us. I miss him dearly and I will always be thankful for that special time that we shared together.

My thanks to Gary for his tireless work in putting together this family treasure on the life of my father, Charlie Lelonek, for our entire family to share. It is truly a priceless gift to all of us.

CHAPTER 3

THE LELONEK FAMILY

Shayah (Shayah Zeile, Yeshayahu, Charles) Lelonek was born on Friday, June 12, 1914, in Sierpc, Poland to Yitzchak Mayer Lelonek of Sierpc and Pesa Baila Kadecka of Biezun. Yitzchak Mayer and Pesa had seven children; Bluma, Shayah, Chaim, Miriam Mania, Moshe Rueven, Tova and Tzvi Hersch.

The Lelonek family was active in their community. During the 1880s and 1890s the "Psalms Society" prayed in the house of Avraham Hersch Lelonek (Yitzchak Mayer's father). The Lelonek house was next to the synagogue and the property in that area was called Hornes Gitter (Horn's properties). Hornes Gitter was managed by Melech Berlinski and Avraham Hersch Lelonek.[29] Bluma Lazinsky, Yitzchak Mayer and Pesa's oldest child, remembered hearing the Purim scroll read in her grandparent's home, Miriam and Avraham Hersch Lelonek. Yitzchak Mayer was a strong Zionist and instilled a love of the Land of Israel in his household. Unsatisfied with the local Jewish education of the cheder or the gymnasium, Yitzchak Mayer Lelonek hired a

---

[29] Talmi, E., (1959) *Kehilat Sierpc; Sefer Zikaron*, Tel Aviv, Israel.
Talmi, E., Krisch, S., Lipsky, D. K., Landau, J., & Weingarten, A. (2014). *Memorial Book of Sierpc, Poland: Translation of Kehilat Sierpc; Sefer Zikaron*. New York: JewishGen.

private Judaic studies tutor for Charlie. Seeing the educational vacuum for a school which melded a love of Israel, Hebrew language, and Torah studies, Yitzchak Mayer worked with other members of the community to raise funds and establish a Yehuda school. He recruited teachers from Lithuania. Moshe Lelonek was in the first graduating class. The Lelonek children were active in the community's Zionist youth groups. Miriam participated in the HaNoar HaTzioni, the Young Zionists. Tova and Charlie were members of HaShomer HaTzair, the Youth Guard. The Lelonek and Kadecki families were tailors in Sierpc and Biezun.

The Holocaust brought my family's 800-year presence in Poland to an end. Pesa Kadecka was the youngest of nine children. Six of her older siblings had emigrated to New York and Massachusetts between 1890 and the 1920s. Pesa's brother, Yechezkel Kadecki, the community's chazzan,[30] his children, and grandchildren were living in Sierpc at the time of the war and were murdered in the Holocaust. Yitzchak Mayer was the second youngest of at least five children. Aside from Yitzchak and Pesa's family, most of the Leloneks were murdered.[31][32][33] The only surviving family members were a first cousin, Moshe Lelonek, who immigrated to Argentina in the 1920s and a second cousin, Jean Gordon (Gitel Lelonek), who survived by being hidden by a Polish farmer, and lived in Minneapolis.[34] At the outset of the war, Yitzchak Mayer was 55, Pesa was 52, Bluma was 27 and married to David Lazinsky 43, Charlie Shayah was 25, Chaim was 22, Miriam was 19, Moshe was 17 and Tzvi was 14. They were living in Sierpc, Poland. Tova immigrated to Palestine in the 1935. In 1980, Charlie was 66 and living in Brooklyn, NY when he was interviewed by his son David, who was 21, for the Holocaust class assignment.

---

[30] Prayer leader.
[31] Lelonek, S., (1948) *Zaml Book Fun Sierpcer Shairit HaChurban.* Sierpcer Jewish Committee (US Zone Germany.)
[32] Yad Vashem Daf Ed, Charlie Lelonek.
[33] Yad Vashem Daf Ed, Bluma Lazinsky.
[34] http://www.wisconsinhistory.org/HolocaustSurvivors/Gordon.asp

PART II

CHARLIE LELONEK'S TESTIMONY

DAVID LELONEK'S INTERVIEW OF CHARLIE

CHAPTER 4

JEWISH LIFE IN SIERPC

Charlie: I was born in Poland. The name of the town is Sierpc, it's about 130 km *(79 miles NW)* from Warsaw. It was a nice Jewish town. The town was full of Jewish life. Many, many Jewish organizations. Many, many Jewish history came from that town. I just like to mention a few, which is still fresh in my mind, as I have been away from the town since 1939. We have there a very educated, lively Jewish society. And within all Jewish organizations, which took part and enriched these all Jewish life in our town. Very, very big group, namely the Zionist, which was split up into different factions, HaNoar HaTzioni, HaShomer HaTzair, the general Zionist group which was located in the center of town. And there was a very, very big library, which supplied all our Jewish younger people with books, knowledge, literature, education and all other aspects of Jewish life. The library contained books in Polish language, also Jewish language, in all the different languages.

The people in our town, mostly middle-class people, were living a quiet normal Jewish life essentially. I like to let you know, my son, that going back, in researching the story of our family, which was a very, very old resident, namely the family Lelonek, was living in that town more than 800 years according to the record. The Lelonek family occupied a house, a very old house near the big shul. The house was over 250 years. And all the engineers from that time came down to see the structure, the layout and the building material which were put in that house. The house went over from generation to generation, for a couple hundred years until the war. Before the war, the Lelonek family donated that house to the Jewish community center, to the Jewish Gominda calling it. They erased the house and in that place, they want to build a parking lot for the younger people to play. Of course, at that point, the war came and nothing happened. The shul was destroyed, together with the Jewish people in that town.

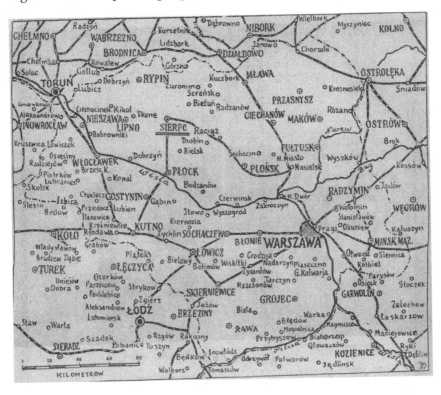

Map of Sierpc circa 1939. Source: *Kehilat Sierpc; Sefer Zikaron.* The Jews of Sierpc were transported from Sierpc to Nowy Dwór (N. Dwór) to Warsaw. Pesa Lelonek's hometown, Biezun, is 22 km NE of Sierpc.

CHAPTER 5

INVASION OF POLAND

Charlie: I like to start to tell you what happened in our town when the war started.[35][36] *(See Historical Context: Invasion of Poland)* In particular, when the town came to an end of its existence without the Jewish people. Sometime in November 1939, after the war started and the Germans occupied the town, the feeling was that something bad will happen and the fear of the people was very, very great. Of course, no one know what's coming. Everyone, since the war broke out, sitting in the house. No one could go out for his, their normal function. The Germans on their part, started to react violently, brutal to the Jewish people in town. I just like to mention, that before that date of November 1939, a lot of miserable things happened in town. For example, right after the Germans occupied Poland, and they went, they came into Sierpc, they collected all the younger people inside, and grabbed them from the street, put them in jail, latter they put them on buses and trucks, brought to Russia frontier and let them out and

---

[35] Charlie Lelonek's account of the events in Sierpc is consistent with the history recorded in The United States Holocaust Memorial Museum Encyclopedia of Camps and Ghettos, 1933-1945: Ghettos in German-Occupied Eastern Europe, page 27
[36] Talmi, E., (1959) *Kehilat Sierpc; Sefer Zikaron*, Tel Aviv, Israel.
Talmi, E., Krisch, S., Lipsky, D. K., Landau, J., & Weingarten, A. (2014). *Memorial Book of Sierpc, Poland: Translation of Kehilat Sierpc; Sefer Zikaron*. New York: JewishGen.

dumped them. Everyone thought that these men were killed. Afterward, after war we found out they didn't kill them, they just let them out and throw them over to the Soviets.

David: Were these people from Sierpc?

Charlie: Yes. From that date on, the life, the general life, daily life, was a matter only of existence. No more, no more normal life. The Germans grabbed the Jewish people from the homes, broke doors into houses, grabbed people from hiding places and put them to work, wherever they feel, they felt having fun of Jewish labor.

Historical Context: Invasion of Poland

Germany and the Soviet Union signed the Treaty of Non-Aggression, First Molotov–Ribbentrop Pact, in Moscow on August 23, 1939. The agreement gave Hitler the go ahead to invade Poland and guaranteed Nazi Germany that they would not have to fight the USSR. The Soviet Union would take part in the invasion of Poland and its subsequent dismemberment.

On August 25, 1939, Britain and Poland signed Agreement of Mutual Assistance. The agreement contained promises of mutual military assistance between the nations in the event some "European country" attacked either. Britain, sensing a dangerous trend of German expansionism, sought to prevent German aggression by this show of solidarity. In a secret protocol of the pact, Britain offered assistance in the case of a German attack on Poland. Because of the pact's signing, Hitler postponed his planned invasion of Poland from August 26, 1939, until September 1, 1939.

The invasion of Poland by Germany and the Soviet Union marked the beginning of World War II in Europe. The German invasion began on September 1, 1939, one week after the signing of the Molotov-Ribbentrop Pact, while the Soviet invasion commenced on September 17, 1939. The Germans reached Sierpc on September 8, 1939. The campaign ended on October 6, 1939, with Germany and the Soviet Union dividing and annexing Poland. In the Soviet-controlled territory, approximately 2 million Polish citizens (including a quarter of a million POWs and 1.5 million deportees) were arrested and imprisoned by the NKVD and other Soviet authorities. On September 3, 1939, British Prime Minister Chamberlain went to the airwaves to announce to the British people that a state of war existed between their country and Germany. World War II had begun.

As I know, the most horrible thing was in Yom Kippur, 1939 (*September 23, 1939[37]*). They grabbed the chazzan (*Charlie's uncle, Yechezkel Kadecki, was the community prayer leader. He was beaten and his beard cut off.[38]*), the shochet,[39] and a couple very, very religious men from town. Of course, the Germans knew that it is Yom Kippur. They make them sweep the market, which was in center of town, all day long and then they threw the garbage back on the street and they make them sweep again until the night and then they released all these people. Imagine, such a religious people, as the chazzan, the shochet, very, very orthodox Jews, which were used to give away the day for prayer and they worked all day with garbage, straw, dirt without a stop and the Germans were standing over them, making fun of them, and didn't let them go until the night.

After that, other things came into existence. Namely, there was a decree that all Jewish people, which likes, which like to venture out on the street must wear a yellow star. Of course, not everyone could take it. Only, whoever went out without a yellow star, was apprehended. (*See Historical Context: Expulsion from the Countryside and the Yellow Star*) The Germans gave them a very big beating, they bruised him, hit him over the head, and put him to jail. And this people, which wore the star and ventured out on the street, were grabbed, put into work, unnecessary work, and beaten up too and let them down, making such ugly things to them, that people were afraid from going out altogether. Only, how he can live in town without going out? It was a need to look for food, for all the necessities, which people must venture into the street in obtaining. In the middle of the holiday season, the Germans brought in, in Sierpc a couple hundred Jewish young men from all the towns surrounding Sierpc. They brought them in, in a big factory, which was abandoned before the war, namely the Shajanka. There, the

---

[37] Talmi, E., (1959) *Kehilat Sierpc; Sefer Zikaron*, Tel Aviv, Israel.
Talmi, E., Krisch, S., Lipsky, D. K., Landau, J., & Weingarten, A. (2014). *Memorial Book of Sierpc, Poland: Translation of Kehilat Sierpc; Sefer Zikaron*. New York: JewishGen.
[38] Talmi, E., (1959) *Kehilat Sierpc; Sefer Zikaron*, Tel Aviv, Israel. p. 424, 457
[39] Kosher butcher.

Historical Context: Expulsion from the Countryside and the Yellow Star

After the invasion of Poland, 2.2 million of Poland's 3.5 million Jews lived in the German partition of Poland. On September 21, 1939, a conference was held to discuss the long-term future of Polish Jewry. Reinhard Heydrich, the Chief of the Reich Central Security Office, reported that as a "prerequisite of the ultimate aim," all Jews were to be concentrated in the larger cities and large areas of western Poland "should be cleared completely of Jews."

After Yom Kippur, September 23, 1939, the Jews of Sierpc were ordered to wear a yellow badge with the word "Jude" on the left side. On October 12, 1939, Hans Frank was appointed Governor-general over German-occupied Poland. On November 23, 1939, Hans Frank announced from Krakow "All Jews and Jewesses over the age of 11 throughout the General Government must wear a four-inch armband in white, marked with the star of Zion on the right sleeve of their inner and outer clothing."

Germans put in the people from Dobzryń, Rachaj, Zuromin and other smaller towns and they let them stay there without any sanitary conditions, without sleeping mattresses, without blankets. The Jewish people from Sierpc got notice of that. We, all together, started to collect food, as little food as was between the Jewish people in the wartime already, we shared our food with a couple hundred young men. And only there was permitted to come up, was young ladies. Young ladies brought in the food. They had to put the food in before the gate of the abandoned factory and they let a couple of young men come out and bring in the food. After a while, they took these young men, the Germans, and put them on buses and trucks and brought them out for unknown destination.

The big trouble started one day in November, it was the day of Simchat Torah[40] night when the Germans put the synagogue on fire. In that night, the Germans were knocking on the door of all Jewish homes around the synagogue, and they were screaming "your temple is on fire, go out and save it." And whoever went out got arrested. It

---

[40] The holiday following Sukkot, celebrating the completion of the yearly cycle of reading the Torah, bible.

was a ruse. A couple of people were shot to death because they ventured out of the house with pails of water to save the synagogue. The Germans having fun of these things, took all the opportunities to bring down the spirit of the Jewish people and make their lives very, very miserable until November. It is my recollection, it was November 12, 1939,[41] the town was awaken very early in the morning, it was 5 or 6 o'clock in the morning. They brought all the people; young, old, children, infants, and sick ones out in the middle in the marketplace in the town. There, they were keeping them for a couple hours until midday, in which a procession of immigration in sorrow (?) pushed all the 6,000 Jewish souls right to the station, railroad station, which was in the end of town. There, they ordered all the Jewish people in cattle cars and the destination was unknown. After riding all day, the people arrived in the town of Nowy Dwór, which is about 80 to 90 km *(89 km/56 miles SE)* from Sierpc.

David: You were in this also?

Charlie: There, they let the people out and chased them over a bridge. Which was the bridge over Buk Narew.[42] This was presumably was the frontier, which should establish a borderline between annexation of Prussian, of Poland to Germany. In the other part, occupation part of Poland, which Warsaw as the center city in Poland. Imagine the situation, in the night when 6,000 people were let out, from the, how you call it, cars, animal cars. Yes?

David: Yeah.

Charlie: The panic. The fear. The confusion. People were screaming, crying. Mothers lost their children. Fathers lost their wives.

---

[41] November 8, 1939 according to the accounts in the *Kehilat Sierpc; Sefer Zikaron*, p, 423, 431. There are discrepancies regarding the date. One survivor (p. 423) recalled that it was a Monday, which would be more consistent with Charlie's date. The Jews of Sierpc traveled through Nowy Dwór and over the next 10 days made their way into Warsaw.

[42] In Nowy Dwór there is a river called "Narew."

The Sierpc Synagogue. Source: *Kehilat Sierpc; Sefer Zikaron*

And the Germans behind were pushing the people, and pushing them with bayonets, hitting them over the body, over the head, and tell them to run fast over the bridge. And every one of us running fast over the bridge until we come over on the other side. On the other side was a little tiny town, Nowy Dwór, and we, all the people, all of us knocking on doors, and asking for pity "let us in, let us in." And the people opened their doors and they let us in.

Soon, it got daytime, we saw that we are still in Poland. We didn't know even where we were. We thought we were someplace in the wilderness. From there, everyone, of the remnant of the town, went into Warsaw *(35.3 km/22 miles SE from Nowy Dwór, November 1939[43])*, where the city was big and the population was heavy. And we was, and everyone was, looking for refuge; where to go, where to start, how to live and how to survive.

---

[43] ITS inquiry card (31408151-0-1). Courtesy of USHMM.

CHAPTER 6

EXILE TO SIBERIA

Charlie: I was with the family, when we came back in Warsaw, without any means of financially, without any clothing, without any hope. We have some distant relatives in Warsaw, which were living in town. And I knew the direction. I went with the family there and told them the story of what happened to us. That, we lost our home, we were distressed, we didn't have anymore, the town is empty, we can't go back. And these people, the distant relatives, gave us refuge. They told us, in that building, there is one empty apartment and the people moved out. We can take it and start rebuilding our lives. Of course, it was very, very pleasant to come in, in the house, which was more or less a home. There were blankets, pillows, dishes. The house wasn't clean but it was a roof. And the family started to resettle in this new quarters. So it was my father, my mother, it was my brother Chaim,[44] my brother Moshe, my sister Bluma, my sister Miriam, and my brother-in-law Lazinsky, David. Also, there were near us a couple friends which we took in for pity because they didn't have where to go. From there

---

[44] Bluma Lazinsky documents her brother's, Chaim Lelonek, death on the Yad Vashem Daf Ed. She records that he was single, b. 1917 and died at 25 years old (1942). He was captured and lost at the beginning of the war in Russia. The family lived at 7 Daszynskiego Rd, Sierpc, Poland.

we started to think what to do next, how to organize a new life in the big city, which was also occupied by the Germans. The life in Warsaw wasn't a paradise. The same thing was happened in the small towns, happened in the big city. The German were grabbing people from the street and put them to work. Some of them came back, some of them never came back. And it was rumors that one day the Germans will create a ghetto in Warsaw. The fear, that they would put in the people in a ghetto, was even greater than any other thing. Because we knew, that a ghetto it is a closed in thing, where you can only go in and you can't go out to leave. In a ghetto in, and outside are enemies like the German Nazis. We thought it is a danger, that one day something very, very bad will happen. They can take us all out from the ghetto in one day and destroy us. And fear of that was in our heart. And we were very much afraid. And we heard, that in the other side of the border, not far from Warsaw, about 150 km *(195 km/121 miles NE)*, there is the Soviet occupation of Poland, namely the city of Bialystok *(See Historical Context: Division of Poland[45])*. That the Jewish life is going on, largely normal with the Soviet occupation and troops. All we decided, that the best thing it will be, to go over there and see what's happening...So me, my brother and sister, 3 of us...

David: Which one?

Charlie: Moshe and Miriam, we took the train and went over to the frontier...and cross the border, we came into Bialystok. There, the conditions we found were very poorly. The people were living in squalor all over the place in the synagogue and in different places of communal living. But no place was there to go because the population of Bialystok was very heavy. And the residents of the town Bialystok were very unfriendly to the slew of refugees from the different parts of the country. They were afraid that we will bring diseases, crime and other things, which was a natural fear. Only besides fear and

---

[45] The Treaty of Non-Aggression between Germany and the Soviet Union. http://www.britannica.com/EBchecked/topic/230972/German-Soviet-Nonaggression-Pact

discomfort, life was going on as normal. Jewish people didn't behave like they were a pig or something. Different people ventured out in the street, they were conducting business, much enjoying themselves, no one was arrested, no one was disturbed. Seeing that life is possible on this side of the border with the Russian people, we decided the best thing is to go back and bring back the parents and let them have a secure life, with these people, which are not taking advantage of our Jewishness. So I decided myself, with my other brother, that all of us cannot go back because we have no financial means. I sold a couple of my personal belongings, for a couple of dollars, and I ventured back to the frontier, I came back to Warsaw *(195 km/121 miles SW)*.

David: Was it hard to get back there?

Charlie: It was very, very dangerous undertaking. First of all, I had to cross the Soviet frontier. Going to the German frontier, and then to venture on a train, which was always checked by the Germans, the SS, and Gestapo, they keeping throwing out Jewish people. And then to

Historical Context: Division of Poland

Second Ribbentrop–Molotov Pact of September 28, 1939. Map of Poland signed by Stalin and Ribbentrop adjusting the German-Soviet border in the aftermath of German and Soviet invasion of Poland. Note that Warschau (Warsaw) is in German territory and Bialystok is in Soviet territory.

27

arrive to Warsaw, from where I have to venture out to the bridges, to town, until I arrive to the place where my folks are. I came back to my folks and I told them what I saw on the other side of the frontier. That Jewish people living in the Russian side and they seem not so concerned and didn't have too much fear. No one is bothering them. I was sitting with mine parents and discussing with them the importance of survival for several days. Let you understand the Jewish people, with ties with tradition, with the religion, and the idea that the Soviets are communist dominated people. The fear for my father and mother, that they will not hold onto the tradition life, we will not be able to preserve the Jewish life, was an obstacle and they refused to go along. Only, I was trying to persuade them, day by day, hour by hour, night and day, that the most important aspect of life is survival. Regardless of the condition, religion, political or other things, survival of your own personal life is the strongest thing. After 4, 5 days I persuaded them. They said "Well, we will try. I will take my tallis,[46] my tefillin."[47] And my father said, "and we will try to see what's going on there." *(See Historical Context: Leaving Europe in the Face of the Rise of Nazi Anti-Semitism)* I took my father, my mother and we obtained railroad tickets and we came in to the frontier.

David: Was it hard to get out of Warsaw?

Charlie: It was very hard and very dangerous voyage. First of all, I have to bribe, bribe a conductor he should hide us in the wagon because the Germans were checking and throwing out Jewish people. So I paid 50 zloty to a conductor and he hid away all of us in a special coupe, which mean a special section of the train, where the door was

---

[46] Four cornered prayer shawl with strings tied around the corners worn during the prayer service.

[47] Phylacteries are two small black boxes containing specific biblical texts written on parchment. Using long black painted leather straps, one box is wound around the non-dominant arm with the box facing the heart and the other box wound around the head during the daily morning prayer services. They symbolize serving G-d with one's heart and mind.

closed. And he said, the conductor said, "there is no one in, it's closed up." We arrived in the station Malkina *(98.3 km/68 miles NE)*.[48] There, the Germans were waiting for us, the Gestapo and SS And they was screaming and hollering that we are communist, that we going over to the Russian side. And they was beating everyone over the head, over.

Historical Context: Leaving Europe in the Face of the Rise of Nazi Anti-Semitism

Jews living in Europe in the 1930s faced the difficult decision whether to emigrate. Anti-Semitism was rising and the Nazis were running a political platform steeped in anti-Semitism. By November 1938 the Nazis had demonstrated little regard for Jewish life. The implications of the rise the Nazis was not yet clear for Europe. In his testimony, Charles Lelonek discusses the main issues that form the basis of the emigration question.

Historical perspective: The Lelonek family lived in Poland for 800 years and in the same house for 250 years. They had experienced multiple anti-Semitic regimes and wars over the centuries. Many Jews felt secure in their connection to their town and government and that they could weather-the-storm.

Where to go? At the Evian Conference in July 1938, 32 nations gathered together to formulate a policy addressing the refugee crisis of the German Jews who were trying to flee. At the end of the conference, 31 countries did not change their immigration policies, including the US. Only the Dominican Republic opened their immigration quotas. There were very few destinations for those Jews considering immigration. Even for the existing immigration quotas, the immigration requirements were very strict and it was impossible for refugees to obtain government documents like passports and visas when their governments were no longer extant. In the White Paper of May 1939, the British government rejected establishing an independent Jewish state and severely restricted future Jewish immigration to Palestine.

Communism versus Nazi anti-Semitism? For the Jews of Poland, their choice was Nazi anti-Semitism or Stalin's notorious barbaric mistreatment of his own people, anti-Semitic policies, and communism. Stalin was responsible for at least 20 million deaths in the Soviet Union. Russia had a history of government sponsored pogroms of the Jews in the 1880s. Those pogroms led to two million Jews fleeing the Russian Empire between 1880 and 1914. Polish Jews were aware of the Nazi anti-Semitism from their policies in Germany and Austria. The Nazi-sponsored pogrom, Kristallnacht, on November 9-10 1938, spread into Sierpc, with the local anti-Semitic party blocking entrance to Jewish businesses and

---

[48] There is a town Malkina Gorna, Poland between Warsaw and Bialystok.

29

Historical Context Continued: Leaving Europe in the Face of the Rise of Nazi Anti-Semitism

telling the Jewish inhabitants that the "German are coming." After the Nazi invasion of Poland, the Nazis publicly humiliated Jewish leaders. On Yom Kippur, the Nazis publicly beat and cut off the beard of Charlie's uncle, Yechezkel Kadecki, a prayer leader in the community. In November 1939, on Simchat Torah, the Nazis burned the synagogue and murdered a young man who attempted to save the Torah scrolls.

Leave now or wait and see? Before the Nazis invaded Poland in September 1939, the Polish government had signed the Agreement of Mutual Assistance with England to protect it from invasion. At the opening of World War II, the Polish government believed that England would be able to push back the Nazi offensive and that the invasion would only be temporary. Leaving Poland at the outset of the war meant forfeiting family history, possessions, homes and businesses. Even the Jews evicted from the countryside by November 1939, still held on to the hope that they would be able to return to their homes soon and rightfully claim what was their property.

Crossing the Frontier: Crossing the frontier was a difficult and dangerous undertaking. Despite the non-aggression treaty signed between Nazis and the Soviets, the frontier was dangerous. The Nazis and the Soviets did not want refugees crossing the border. Special visas were required to cross the border, officials needed to be bribed and the border secretly crossed. Illegally crossing the border meant risking being beaten and imprisoned by the Nazis or sent to the Gulag by the NKVD. Many refugees were stuck in the forest at the border, waiting to escape to the Soviet Union for several months. In the forest, they faced the challenge of wintry conditions, hunger and lack of medical supplies.

The Lelonek family decided that the risk of staying in Nazi occupied Poland was greater than the risk of leaving their processions behind, crossing the border and facing the uncertainty of Stalin and communism. They withstood the temptation to return to Warsaw while they waited for up to 2 months at the frontier in the forest, living through starvation and the wintry conditions. Their perseverance and decisive nature saved them. They left before the Warsaw Ghetto was established and the Nazis sealed the Jewish population inside in October-November 1940. Had the Lelonek family waited, they would have been trapped in the Ghetto and the Soviet-German border would have been secured making the journey impossible.

the back and chasing us. I got bruised up. I got hit a couple times. And my mother was almost fainting, she got so scared.[49] Finally, we arrived onto the frontier. We came to a neutral zone, between the Russians and the Germans. There, we was sitting for a couple days, in that neutral zone which was in someplace in nowhere, in the wildness. Rain was coming on us. It was way… late… November, in the beginning of December. Rain was coming on us. Snow. Frost. And the people were sitting all together, wrapped in shmatas,[50] in blankets and waiting for a miracle; when the Soviets, will open the barriers and let these hundred or thousand refugees cross the frontier, let them in. And finally, that thing happened. One morning, the Soviets opened the barriers and let all these mass humanities cross. And then, all of them cross the frontier and went over to the next railroad station and we arrived in Bialystok. Safely, we were very happy. The family was reunited. And we came into the synagogue on the Fabryczna Street. The synagogue on Fabryczna Street was located in the poor section of Bialystok. There, was a lot of people from my town. And that was a common quarter for living for a period of months. Let you imagine how a synagogue looks and you bring in a couple hundred of people. The benches in the synagogue, as you know, are big wooden benches, and they are lined up in a certain way, so only for sitting purposes. Instead, we came in and used that for living quarters! So every family which was there, made rearrangement, move around the benches and made separation. Let's say in that section was living the Lelonek family, in another section was living the Singer family and in another section was living the Greener family and so on and so on and so on. And it was 20, 30 families and everyone has a section between, a space between the benches. The benches were turned around in certain a way that we should have a little bit privacy.

---

[49] Bluma Lazinsky records "At the crossing of the line demarcation I have been mistreated heavily by uniformed Germans and was hit with a heavy metal stick on the fingers of my left hand, was heavily wounded and did put a bandage." Bluma Lazinsky reparations request from Germany, January 24, 1964.
[50] Rags.

David: About how much room did a family have?

Charlie: The family room was, well let's say 10 by 10, 10 by 12, 10 by 14 feet.

David: For the whole family?

Charlie: Yes. At night, we laid down, one by one, one by one, like herring. Made packed in. In the morning, everything was covered up. And the people, the people were going on about their business. Of course, the conditions in that shul on Fabryczna Street was not too sanitary. For the upper part of the woman's section only 2 toilet and the bottom part, in the sanctuary was 2 toilets. And there...

(Editor's note: The recording is interrupted and a segment is missing. The following has been reconstructed based on records:

In 1940, while the family was in Bialystok, Chaim was arrested by the Russians and was never heard from again. Chaim appears on the list of cases under investigation by the NKVD's Western Ukrainian and Belarussian apparatus.[51] [52]

Moshe Lelonek, Charlie's younger brother, described what happened in Bialystok;

After the occupation of Poland, they drove us out of our town; we boarded the train to Warsaw and stayed there until they began to concentrate Jews in

---

[51] Karta Index, volume 410, page 84, no. 13. The list contains the following information concerning Chaim Lelonek: register number (887,564), surname (Lelenek), name (Chaim), father's name (Icek), year of birth (1917), investigation number (79,171), and the year of arrest (1940).
http://www.indeks.karta.org.pl/en/szczegoly.jsp?id=79237
[52] Bluma Lazinsky documents her brother, Chaim Lelonek's death on the Yad Vashem Daf Ed. She records that he was single, b. 1917 and died at about 25 years old (1942). He was captured and lost at the beginning of the war in Russia. The family lived at 7 Daszynskiego Rd, Sierpc, Poland. He was a tailor.

ghettos. My brother *(Charlie)* and I took backpacks and fled to Bialystok, where we were for a number of months. After several months, in the early morning, the secret police came to our house and told us to come out, they are taking us somewhere. Outside was a van that took us to the train station in the city. They put us on train carriages, which were cattle cars. After a four-week train ride to the northern Russia cities in Arkhangelsk *(Siberia),* we were housed in barracks in the woods. We worked cutting wood in the forest and in return every day we received bread and soup. The temperature was 45 degrees below 0.[53]

Bluma, Charlie's older sister, writes in her reparation request;

> We were arrested by the Russians for illegally crossing the line of demarcation and dragged to Siberia. At the crossing of the line demarcation I was mistreated heavily by uniformed Germans and was hit with a heavy metal stick on the fingers of my left hand, was badly wounded. I bandaged *(my wound)*.

> In Siberia, there was no medical help, and my wound was not treated medically. Since that time, my left hand is crippled. Then we were brought to the Arkhangelsk Oblast where my husband was forced to do heavy work in the labor camp, Poyaminka. We constantly were suffering from hunger, heavy cold and humidity.

> The lodging and the clothing situation were terrible.

---

[53] Written by Moshe Lelonek for his great grandchildren's "roots work." Courtesy of his grandson, Oren Yagoda. 2011.

The moral and bodily burdening were very heavy.[54] [55]

According to deportation documents, on July 7, 1940, Itsek *(Yitzchak Mayer)*, Pesa, Shayah *(Charlie)*, Motel *(Miriam)*, Monek *(Moshe)*, Hersch *(Tzvi)* Lelonek,[56] David and Bluma Lazinsky[57] were banished by the Russians from Bialystok to Arkhangelsk region, Kargopol district, Poyaminka, SALT.[58] A 1,688 km/1,049 miles journey NE into Siberia. The family lived in Siberia for over a year.

The interview continues after the missing audio.)

Charlie: …covered the white nights from the north. In beginning people couldn't get used to it because it was always day. The people suffered tremendous headaches. From there, they ordered the people on trucks and they brought them in deep, deep in the woods, about 150 miles deep in the woods. There were camps, special camps, arranged for people which have political sins or political dissidents. And the families and the single people arrived there, and they were resettled in small little housing, and everyone has to, was mobilized to work the berg. The berg was like these throwing down trees in the

---

[54] Bluma Lazinsky reparation request from Germany, January 24, 1964.

[55] The Soviets used deportations as a means of quashing the conquered society's resistance. They carried out 5 main deportations of 1.5 million Polish citizens in their newly captured territory. Charlie and his family were arrested during the fourth deportations at the end of June through the first week of July 1940. This deportation consisted of 79,000 people who were considered "resettler-refugees." They remained under the control of the NKVD and were stripped of their basic civil right. Source: *Together Forever: The Soviet Occupation of Eastern Poland During World War II.* by Daniel Bockowski.

[56] http://www.indeks.karta.org.pl/en/wyszukiwanie.jsp Search for Lelenek in the surname field. Also listed as being banished the same day to Arkhangelsk are Toba (b. 1919), Cheskel (b. 1920), Frania (b. 1923) Lelenek all listing Icek as their father and Dwojra Lelenek (b.1918) daughter of Juda. All of unknown relation.

[57] http://www.indeks.karta.org.pl/en/szczegoly.jsp?id=232934

[58] Khaia Josefovna Rogozhinski, http://khaja-r.livejournal.com/2923.html The Poyaminka camp is mentioned http://khaja-r.livejournal.com/2955.html She locates Poyaminka a few kilometers from Nyandoma. Nyandoma is in the Arkhangelsk Oblast at 61° 39' 57" N, 40° 11' 49" E. The Arkhangelsk Oblast is an administrative region in Northwestern Russia.

heavy wood, and piled them up, and getting ready for, that wood, for export or for others kinds, they used this. That was going on for about until 1941.

David: (?)

Charlie: The war was going on in Europe. We were in the..., our people were far away from war. We just heard that the Germans attack the Russians. *(The Germans invaded the USSR in Operation Barbarossa on June 21, 1941. See Historical Context: Operation Barbarossa[59])* And they moving, and they taking away portions of Russia. And the Russians have a treaty. Again, being far away from the war, we were starting to fear that the Germans, maybe, can reach us too, far away in the north. The name of that place where we were isolated was Poyaminka, and the region was Arkhangelsk. This was the most northern outlet from the Russian country; it very much to the north, there is never summer, always winter. Nothing is growing, and nothing is blooming, there is only woods and snow and frost. After being there a while, the people started getting sick and scarbut *(scurvy)*. This is a sickness of the skin and of the muscles, people getting black spots, openings in the calves and the back and the hand and they never healed. This was a product of our malnutrition and lack of vitamin C. And it was no remedy, whoever got sick and that one gradually died. In 1941, all of the sudden it was a decree from the Russian government, that all these people which were isolated in the north, should be free all.[60] *(The Lelonek family was granted "special settlement on amnesty" on September 7, 1941.[61])* And let them go wherever they like. Imagine the happiness of us and all the people. And the Russians, after a while, provided transportations, and they gave people a little money and a choice where to go. Our family

[59] Operation Barbarossa, Map courtesy of naval-history.net
http://www.britannica.com/EBchecked/topic/52772/Operation-Barbarossa
[60] Sikorski-Maysky Accord
http://www.britannica.com/EBchecked/topic/466681/Poland/28215/World-War-II
[61] Polish special settlers in the Arkhangelsk region, http://lists.memo.ru

Historical Context: Operation Barbarossa

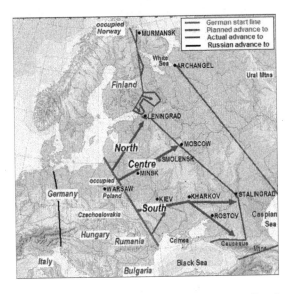

On June 21, 1941, Hitler opened up the Eastern offensive invading the Soviet Union. He intended to reach the far reaches of the Soviet Union, including Arkhangelsk where the Lelonek family was living. Hitler wrote in Mein Kamph that he wanted to invade the Soviet Union, asserting that the German people needed to secure Lebensraum (living space) to ensure the survival of Germany for generations to come. The Germans advanced quickly and successfully but eventually were repelled at Stalingrad, in an epic battle. The loss lead to a war of attrition, which coupled with the Russian winter, became a drain on German resources. The failure of Operation Barbarossa was a turning point in the fortunes of the Third Reich. Most importantly, the operation opened up the Eastern Front, to which more forces were committed than in any other theater of war in world history. The Eastern Front became the site of some of the largest battles, most horrific atrocities, and highest casualties for Soviets and Germans alike. After the German invasion of the Soviet Union, Stalin began to seek help from other countries opposing Germany, including the non-existent Poland. Following the London July 30, 1941, agreement between the Soviet Union and the Polish Government in Exile, the Sikorski-Maysky accord, Stalin agreed to declare all previous pacts he had with Nazi Germany null and void, invalidating the September 1939 Soviet-German Nonaggression Treaty and partition of Poland, and releasing 230,000 Polish prisoners-of-war held in Soviet camps, including the Lelonek family who were detained in Arkhangelsk. Pursuant to an agreement between the Polish government-in-exile and Stalin, the Soviets granted amnesty to all Polish citizens on August 12, 1941.

moved to the town of Gorky.[62] *(889 km/550 miles SE. Today Gorky is called Nizhny Novgorod.[63])* We never knew the town. We just looked on the map, and we saw there is name Gorky. So we decided, it's laying in middle of Russia. Let's go down from the north to the middle of Russia and from there we can move around to a different part, which was a very understandable thing. We wanted to be in the middle of all the happenings. After a couple of weeks, we arrived at Gorky. Gorky was a very, very, busy, busy town. In Gorky is the biggest Russian auto industry. In Gorky was the biggest Russian tank industry. In Gorky was the biggest center of command at that time.

David: Was it far from Moscow?

Charlie: It was 280 miles *(417 km/249 miles)* from Moscow, it lays exactly in center of Russia. In meantime, while we were in Gorky, the Russians *(the war front)* were already almost in Moscow. And the fear of the war, that the Germans would get us again, was coming on us. We were very much afraid. Happened a miracle that the Russians fought back the Germans from Moscow and we were safe for a while.

From there, we were put away in a small town, about 120 miles from Gorky. Of course, the influx of refugees to the city of Gorky was tremendous. In the schools, in the other public buildings were occupied by refugees. And they didn't know what to do with them. So, the Russians then decided to put all the refugees in camps or not in camps exactly, in the farms because there was a very big shortage of farmhands. The men were at war, the woman were alone. So, they figured they would put these people away in farms, collective farms, and these people will work. Our family was put out, away, about 120 miles from Gorky, in the town of Ravinspor. It's really a small village. It was a big, big farm sometimes, which belong to one man and then, when the Soviets took it over, the government convert to a commune

---

[62] Icek and Pesa Lelonek and Hersz "Care and Maintenance; Application for Assistance." International Tracing Service courtesy of USHMM.
[63] http://www.britannica.com/EBchecked/topic/416591/Nizhny-Novgorod

farm. There, the family was given a small little house. And all the people went to work in the fields. Imagine, all the sudden my father, mother, my brothers, which were very young, everyone has to do farm work. We have to handle horses, cows, all kinds of other work which we were never used to do. Only, if life is important to do it, you do it. Whatever was done, no one controlled because there was no man who showed you how to do it. The most work was done by woman and they was teaching us what to do. I, myself, went away from the family and was working in a shop in a town away about 20 miles. In there I was staying for a couple months. I got a little bit refreshed.

David: What town?

Charlie: The town, the name of the town was Vatt,[64] the name of the town was Vatt, the town is on the railroad station between Moscow and the town of Penza. Between Moscow and Penza. That town was a small town and there was a couple of shops. I joined in the shop and was working in the tailor shop. Was like a co-op. There was prepared the pant and jacket, ski jacket, ski pants for the army. I worked there a couple months, until the spring. And then, I looked around and I felt very bad. In the town was only old man over 50 and young girls and old ladies. I was the only man in that shop. It was a very uncomfortable situation. Like I mean to be a stowaway, that meaning... Having a restaurant to eat, I was the only man, male there, there were no other males. Everyone looked at me like I am an outcast.

---

[64] There is a town called Vyksa between Moscow and Penza. It is a 364 km/226 miles from Moscow to Vyksa.

CHAPTER 7

POLISH ARMY IN EXILE

Charlie: Finally, I decided that the condition is not nice. I volunteered for the Goying Komat, this is the Russian army reserve like. *(See Historical Context: Jewish Soldiers in the Allied Armies[65] [66] [67])* In there I went through the formalities, they sent me away, I should join the Polish army which was down forming in the south of Russia near the Iranian border. From there *(Vatt)* I went to Moscow with a group of other Jewish boys, which we met in Moscow. In Moscow, they gave us a transportation route, a special car and we move down south to Kazakhstan, to the town of Alma-Ata. *(3,933 km/2,444 miles SE)* The voyage from Moscow to Alma-Ata took about two months.

David: Around what year was this now?

Charlie: It was 1942.

---

[65]http://www.yadvashem.org/yv/en/holocaust/resource_center/item.asp?gate=2-40

[66] Reprinted with permission from Yad Vashem,
http://www.yadvashem.org/yv/en/holocaust/about/07/jewish_soldiers.asp

[67] Arad, Yitshak. *In the Shadow of the Red Banner: Soviet Jews in the War Against Nazi Germany.* Gefen Publishing House Ltd, 2010

David: Spring, summer?

Charlie: In Alma-Ata[68] it was already the spring. In there, instead being accepted by the army, which the Russians organized for the Polish citizens with the headman of General Sikorski[69] which we should fight for our independence of Poland. It was there a status quo, the people, the officers of that army were very anti-Semitic and they refused to take in too many Jewish people.[70] And the influx of Jewish people was so great, that we got scared because everyone was ready to fight. So finally, after hanging around there for 2, 3 weeks. Where to eat, where to sleep, where to stay, they refused to take into the army. Very disappointed, I have to go back to the north. Went into a train, without any funds, without any knowledge, what to do next and I move back to the north, towards Moscow. *(3,933 km/2,444 miles NW)*

---

[68] Alma-Ata, Kazakhstan.
http://www.britannica.com/EBchecked/topic/16771/Almaty

[69] Władysław Sikorski was a Polish soldier and political figure. After the Polish defeat in the Polish Defensive War of 1939, he became the prime minister of the Polish Government in Exile. Following Operation Barbarossa, he sought to normalize diplomatic relations with the Soviets. The Polish Government reached an agreement with the Soviet Union, the Sikorski-Maysky Pact of August 17, 1941. Stalin agreed to invalidate the September 1939 Soviet-German partition of Poland, declare the Russo-German Molotov-Ribbentrop Pact of August 1939 null and void, and release tens of thousands of Polish prisoners-of-war held in Soviet camps. Pursuant to an agreement between the Polish government-in-exile and Stalin, the Soviets granted "amnesty" to many Polish citizens, from whom a new army (the Polish II Corps, as known as Ander's Army) was formed under General Władysław Anders and later evacuated to the Middle East. Anders Army, like the *Armia Krajowa*, was known to be anti-Semitic. Diplomatic relations deteriorated between the Soviets and the Polish Government in exile after the Germans announced that they had found a mass grave with 20,000 Polish soldiers massacred by the Soviets in Katyn Forest near Smolensk, Russia in April 1943. Sikorski did not accept the Soviet explanation and requested an investigation by the International Red Cross. The Soviets accused the Polish Government in Exile of being allies with the Nazis and broke off diplomatic relations. Sikorski, who continued to favor diplomatic relations with the Soviets, had a conflict with General Anders over normalizing relations with the Soviets. After a visit with General Anders, Sikorski was killed when his plane suspiciously crashed 16 seconds after takeoff. - Wikipedia

[70] Gutman, Yisrael. "Jews in General Anders' Army in the Soviet Union," Shoah Resource Center, The International School for Holocaust Studies, Yad Vashem, http://www.yadvashem.org/odot_pdf/Microsoft%20Word%20-%206564.pdf

Historical Context: Jewish Soldiers in the Allied Armies

Approximately 1.5 million Jews fought in the Allied armies. In many cases, the percentage of Jews fighting was greater than the percentage of Jews in the population.

Approximately 100,000 Jews fought in the Polish army against the German invasion. They made up 10% of the Polish army, commensurate with the percentage of Jews within the general population. Approximately 30,000 Jews fell in battle, were taken captive by the Germans, or declared missing during the battles defending Poland, 11,000 in the defense of Warsaw. Thousands of Jews later served in various Polish armies fighting against the Germans in the Allied Forces.

About 500,000 Jewish soldiers fought in the Red Army during World War II. Some 120,000 were killed in combat and in the line of duty. Over 100,000 Jews from the Red Army were captured by the Nazis, yet few survived. More than 160,000 Jews, at all levels of command, earned citations, with over 150 designated "Heroes of the Soviet Union"- the highest honor awarded to soldiers in the Red Army. In July 1941, after Germany attacked Russia, the Polish People's Army and General Anders Army were allowed to form on Russian soil. Polish refugees, including 17,000-20,000 Polish Jews, joined and fought the Germans alongside the Red Army. Many encountered anti-Semitism and were barred from enlisting based on being a Jew.

Many Jews, including those who managed to escape the Nazi in the late 1930s, served in the armies of the western Allies, especially in the United States and the British armed forces.

Approximately 550,000 Jewish soldiers fought in the US Armed Forces during World War II. They served on all fronts in Europe and in the Pacific. Some 10,000 were killed in combat, and more than 36,000 received citations. Many Jewish soldiers took part in liberating the concentration camps.

Arriving in Moscow, again, I decided to find my family, which I left behind. After a couple of weeks looking for them, I found out they moved to a different place, and I came back to them. We were reunited. And I was staying with them a while.

David: Where were they now?

Charlie: They working in the farms in Russia in the same vicinity. On a different farm. In meantime, something happened. The Russian organized another army of Polish citizens. And this was organized in the name of Wanda Wasilewska,[71] a Polish leader, a lady, which was proclaiming in her proclamation that they seeking all kinds of Polish citizens, which like to fight to liberate a democratic Poland. Listening to that proclamation in the radio, I left again my folks and I came back to the point of destination, which was someplace near Rosayne, about 180 mile from Moscow. From there, they transported us to the concentration point; from there I met again with a lot of Jewish people, which were ready to join that army. The Army of Liberation of Poland, under the leadership of Wanda Wasilewska, we should fight for a democratic and free Poland.[72] We were very happy seeing so many Polish citizens, which were ready to fight for Poland, for a democratic Poland. There, they took us in, in army camps, they started to train us for the war. The Russians, they have in that time advanced war techniques, which they had adapted from the Americans, which they learned from the German, and they was training us for better soldiers. After the training, between 5 and 6 months in the camps, army camps, we left the camps and started to move towards the front. The front was at that time in the Ukraine, near Kiev. After a couple days traveling, we have our unit, we traveled in trains, army trains, we stopped in Kiev, from Kiev we moved to Kharkov *(Kharkov was liberated August 23, 1943. Charlie's stops were Moscow to Kharkov, 739 km/459 miles, and then to Kiev 478 km/297 miles.)*, and from there, we went in, gradually, in combat. We have, in that time, 3 Polish divisions. The

---

71 Wanda Wasilewska was a Polish communist who, prior to the war, served in the Polish Socialist Party. After the Polish defeat in the Polish Defensive War of 1939 and the partition of Poland between Soviets and Germans, she moved to Lviv where she automatically became a Soviet citizen. She founded the Union of Polish Patriots, and sought to have Poland be a part of Russia. In 1943, with direction from Stalin, she initiated the creation of the Polish Army, infantry division, a division of the Soviet Red Army. Her political association was adversarial to the Polish Government in Exile. -Wikipedia

72 Charlie is documented as having joined the Polish People's Army and returned to Poland in the Yizkor book *Kehilat Sierpc; Sefer Zikaron.*

army was a consolidation of all Polish citizens. I would say that it was at least 40% Jewish boys. The high command was Russian, the lower command was Polish. In the lower command were a lot of Jewish officers. In the soldiers, in every unit were a lot of Jewish boys. My squadron was 42 guys, was at least 18 boys, Jewish boys. We felt we much at home, we was talking Yiddish, was talking Polish, and talking Russian. And the feeling was, that we really fighting for a right cause because there was no other way how to do it. Only fight and destroy the enemy. And so many of us were ready to give our lives.

CHAPTER 8

WARSAW UPRISING

Charlie: After a while, we reached the front and they put us in combat. We crossed over the old Polish frontier, near Kovel *(448 km/278 miles W, Kovel was liberated March-April 1944)*, and there we have the first meeting with the enemy. The battles were bitter. We fought like lions. Only, we have one objective in front of us, to destroy the Germans. We decided not to retreat, even when we lose the life, to fight until the last man. From Kovel, we was fighting and pushing the Germans, from one place to the other, from one town to the other. Finally, we reached the city of Lublin, which was in that time a city without Jews already. *(161 km/100 miles W. Lublin was liberated July 24, 1944. See Historical Context: Resistance During the Holocaust[73])* Coming into Lublin, we found out that there was no Jewish people around. Until we reached the first big city, where it was a big Jewish population, we didn't have a clear picture of what happened. Only, coming into Lublin, which was the big yeshiva from Lublin, the big Jewish population, there was so many Jewish synagogues, so many Jewish people, we saw, we didn't see nobody! And we realized what happened

---

[73] United States Holocaust Memorial Museum. "Resistance During the Holocaust." Holocaust Encyclopedia http://www.ushmm.org/m/pdfs/20000831-resistance-bklt.pdf

Historical Context: Resistance During the Holocaust

During World War II an estimated 20,000 to 30,000 Jews fought bravely as partisans in resistance groups that operated under cover of the dense forests of Eastern Europe.

From the Nazis' rise to power in 1933 in Germany to the end of the Third Reich in 1945, Jews participated in many acts of resistance. Organized armed resistance was the most direct form of opposition to the Nazis. In many areas of German-occupied Europe, resistance took other forms such as aid, rescue, and spiritual resistance.

As the victims of Nazi genocide and an isolated, often scorned, minority among occupied populations, Jews were in a distinctively weak situation. Because they were doomed to destruction, they could not wait for the beginning of the German collapse in 1943 to act, as the nationalist and patriotic anti-Nazi resistance movements generally did. By the end of 1942, more than four million Jews had already been killed by mass shootings and gassings or had died from starvation, exhaustion, and disease during their internment in Nazi ghettos and concentration and forced labor camps.

Nazi methods of deception and terror and the superior power of the German police state and military severely inhibited the abilities of civilians in all occupied countries to resist. But the situation of Jews was particularly hopeless, and it is remarkable that individuals and groups resisted to the extent they did.

In addition to many acts of unarmed resistance in the ghettos and camps and the armed and unarmed resistance of Jewish partisans operating underground in both eastern and western Europe, armed Jewish resistance took place in 5 major ghettos, 45 small ghettos, 5 major concentration and extermination camps, and 18 forced labor camps. With few exceptions (notably three major uprisings by partisans in late summer 1944 in Warsaw, Paris, and Slovakia as Allied liberators approached), Jews alone engaged in open, armed resistance against the Germans.

to our people. From Lublin, we fought our way more to the north and our destination was Warsaw; to reach the center of Poland, free the capital of Poland and take over the center city, take over the government and continue to live as a free people together with the Polish people. The time was moving on. Between the combat, from Kovel until Warsaw took about 6 months *(326 km / 202 miles)*. We

arrived near Warsaw about in the month of August, ...1943 (1944[74]).
In combat we met rarely Jewish people, we only met partisans. This is
people, which fought in guerrilla groups. They told us the story, what
had happened to the people. They told us that most people were
destroyed and were sent to the different destruction camps, like
Treblinka, Auschwitz, which was strange to us. They notified us that
all the towns and villages are empty of Jews. That very few people are
left. And these people are left, are only in the woods, which they're
hiding. Most of the people which are left are fighting in groups and the
towns are empty of Jews. To our disappointment, we met very, very
few Jewish people. And we arrived in one part of Warsaw, I mean
Warsaw has two parts. Warsaw inner city and Praga on the other side
of the river Vistula. We arrived in the part in combat, into Praga and
we looked and there we dug in and we saw that Warsaw is burning.
The Germans are trying to set everything on fire. And they want to
give us away nothing. They figure, instead we should take over portions
of the city in good condition, they rather destroy the rest, we should
get nothing. So, our command decided to attack the other part of inner
city of Warsaw on erev Yom Kippur, 1943 *(The Polish People's Army
crossed the Vistula on Rosh HaShanah eve, September 16, 1944.[75] Charlie was
a private rank soldier who fought in the in 9th Infantry Regiment, 3rd Infantry
Division of the Ludowe Wojsko Polskie (Polish People's Army) under General
Zygmunt Berling [76]).* We went and attack. They put us in pontoons, they
see such kind of ships, and they ingenious, put them on the water, we
went in, in them. The Germans was putting out fire; from artillery and
from bazookas, and all kind fire. Whoever got drowned, got killed.

---

[74] Records indicate the Szaja Lelonek fought in the Warsaw Uprising, September
1944.

[75] Records indicate the Szaja Lelonek fought in the Warsaw Uprising, on Rosh
HaShanah eve, September 16, 1944. There are no records of soldiers crossing on
Yom Kippur eve, September 26, 1944. In fact, the army was already in retreat at that
time trying to cross back the Vistula to the Russian controlled side. His last contact
was September 22, 1944.

[76] *Book of the Dead on the Field of Glory: Polish People's Army Soldiers who were Killed, Died
of Wounds and Missing During the Second World War in the Years 1943-1945.* 1974. Page
874.

Whoever survived, come over to the other end. There we were fighting hand to hand, and we establish a bridgehead. Our company, which was 185 boys, arrived on the other side of the water and we lost about 80 people. We was numbering only about 100. There we came over and we dug in ourselves. And we have to move cautiously, to the streets of the town, of the big city of Warsaw, we move in from the dug out to the houses.

David: Was it night?

Charlie: It was at night.

David: Yeah.

Charlie: The night in Yom Kippur, 1943.[77] *(See Historical Context: Warsaw Uprising* [78] [79]*)* And that, with grenades and fire, we push back Germans from a couple streets. Hoping that the Polish army or the Russian *(army)*, which was behind us, would support our objective and give us help and give us new material to alter the bridgehead. Unfortunate, the help didn't come. After two weeks of combat and trouble, without water, without food, without ammunition, the Germans pushed us back to the edge of the river, Vistula. And from that, shot at all our units, all our battalions, many, many friends lost. Most of the people demoralized, dirty, lousy, without ammunition. We was sitting on the edge of the river and surrendered to the Germans after two weeks of combat.

---

[77] Records indicate the Szaja Lelonek fought in the Warsaw Uprising, on Rosh HaShanah eve, September 16, 1944. There are no records of soldiers crossing on Yom Kippur eve, September 26, 1944. In fact, the army was already in retreat at that time trying to cross back the Vistula to the Russian controlled side.

[78] Adapted with permission from Encyclopedia Britannica, © 2016 by Encyclopedia Britannica, Inc. Warsaw Uprising.
http://www.britannica.com/EBchecked/topic/636161/Warsaw-Uprising

[79] http://www.warsawuprising.com/

Historical Context: Warsaw Uprising

The Warsaw Uprising (August 1 - October 2, 1944), was a part of Operation Tempest by the Polish resistance Home Army to liberate Warsaw from the Germans. The plan was for the Poles to oust the German army and seize control of the city before the advancing Soviet army occupied it.

As the Red Army approached Warsaw (July 29 - 30, 1944), Soviet authorities, promising aid, encouraged the Polish underground there to stage an uprising against the Germans. However, the Polish underground, known as the *Armia Krajowa*, the Home Army, was anxious because the Soviet Union had already assumed direct control of eastern Poland and had sponsored the formation of the Polish Committee of National Liberation to administer the remainder of Soviet-occupied Polish territory. Hoping to gain control of Warsaw before the Red Army could "liberate" it; the Home Army followed the Soviet suggestion to revolt.

Commanded by general Tadeusz Bór-Komorowski, the Warsaw corps of 50,000 troops attacked the relatively weak German force on August 1, 1944, and within three days gained control of most of the city. The Germans sent in reinforcements and forced the Poles into a defensive position, bombarding them with air and artillery attacks for the next 63 days.

Meanwhile, the Red Army, which had been detained during the first days of the insurrection by a German assault, occupied a position at Praga, a suburb across the Vistula River from Warsaw, and remained idle. The Red Army reached the Vistula on September 14, 1939. In its ranks was the Ludowe Wojsko Polskie, the Polish People's Army under General Zygmunt Berling, which included Szaja Lelonek, which was understandably anxious to liberate Warsaw. However, Stalin ordered the Red Army to halt on the river. Communications from the Home Army were deliberately ignored by the Soviets and the Soviets did nothing for two days. Under pressure from his western allies, Stalin eventually sent a token force across into Warsaw. On September 16, The Polish People's Army was given the green light to cross the Vistula and three divisions, including Charlie's, were sent into the Czerniakow district. 300 troops from the 3rd Infantry Division crossed the river bringing with them machine-guns, anti-tank guns, and mortars. The badly needed reinforcements bolstered the Home Army Group Radoslaw. Three divisions headed into Warsaw, however only 1,500 troops made it across the river, the rest being cut off by the Germans and destroyed piecemeal on the riverbanks. The remaining Polish troops and equipment were absorbed into local

Historical Context Continued: Warsaw Uprising

Home Army regiments. However, the Soviets did not commit its army, artillery or aircraft to assist the uprising under orders from Stalin. In addition, the Soviet government refused to allow the western Allies to use Soviet air bases to airlift supplies to the beleaguered Poles.

Without Allied support, the Home Army split into small, disconnected units and was forced to surrender when its supplies gave out on October 2, 1944. They surrendered only when the Germans agreed to treat POWs under the laws of the Geneva Convention. Polish general Bór-Komorowski and his forces were taken prisoner, and the Germans then systematically deported the remainder of the city's population and destroyed the city itself.

Meanwhile, the Soviet army waited quietly on the opposite riverbank and the Polish capital remained in German control until January 1, 1945. By allowing the Germans to suppress the Warsaw Uprising, the Soviet authorities also allowed them to eliminate the main body of the military organization that supported the Polish government-in-exile in London. Consequently, when the Soviet army occupied all of Poland, there was little effective organized resistance to its establishing Soviet political domination over the country and imposing the communist-led Provisional Government of Poland.

CHAPTER 9

PRISONER OF WAR

David: Around how many *(prisoners)*?

Charlie: How many? I don't know exactly, only that it was there a couple thousand…*(Szaja Lelonek is listed as having died or gone missing without a trace in Warsaw on September 22, 1944, his last contact with Russian authorities.[80] [81] [82])* The Germans surrounded us, took away our possession, our belts, our document, our personal things, they pushed us out from the combat zone, from there they took us to inner city. They made the Jewish people step in front, whoever stepped out in front, they shot him. I decided to say, not to say nothing, I was keeping my mouth shut and I survived. I went with all the Polacks soldiers to prison. There, was a big confusion, as thousands of Polish war prisoners in the city of Warsaw, the war was going on. Everyone was looking for himself. There were so many wounded Polish soldiers. They were seeking help. No one was giving them, they were dying. The

---

[80] *Book of Buried Polish Soldiers Killed During World War II."* 1993, page 253.

[81] *Book of the Dead on the Field of Glory: Polish People's Army Soldiers who were Killed, Died of Wounds and Missing During the Second World War in the Years 1943-1945."* 1974. Page 874.

[82] *United Illustrated Encyclopedia of the Warsaw Uprising: List of Participants of the Warsaw Uprising Soldiers.* 2002. Page 797.

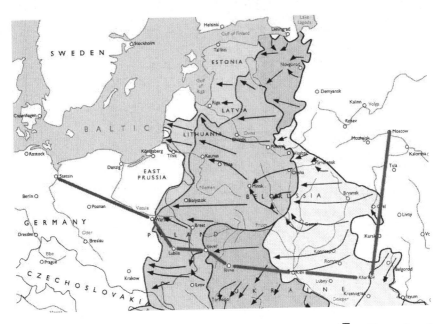

Soviet advances from August 1, 1943 to December 31, 1944: ▢ to December 1, 1943, ▢ to April 30, 1944, ▢ to August 19, 1944, ▢ to December 21, 1944. Charlie's journey as a Polish soldier in the Russian army is highlighted until Warsaw, Poland. Followed by his journey as a prisoner of war to Stettin, Germany.

healthy one was seeking, looking for food, for shelter, for sleep. Finally, the Germans concentrated and collected all these remnants of us. They ordered us, again, on freight cars. And they said; "Destination, Germany." After a couple of days of traveling, we arrived in Stettin. *(559 km/347 miles from Warsaw.)* It's a city in Germany. There they put us in a camp and they started to sort the people for different function. The healthy one, they asking everybody, who is healthy, who is sick, who is tired, who is wounded. The healthy ones they took on one side, and from there, the sick ones they put on another side, the wounded ones they took away in the hospitals. I was the one with the healthy ones of course. There, they took in everyone for a doctor's inspection. They wanted to really, to make sure that the guys are healthy. Every has to disrobe himself naked. They run through inspection. Like, to see if the body is clean, you don't have any kind of sores or the doctor listen to your heart, if you are not sick, it was a very fast procession.

And everyone was screaming, "Schnell, schnell, schnell, schnell, mach schnell!"[83] Of course, I was running, schnell, schnell. And no one looked at me, you know I am Jewish, I am circumcised. No one has time to look. I running fast, one doctor back to the other. Finally, I reached the destination. And I get my clothing back. And the doctor listened to my heart and said: "It is good." And I can go to work. So, from there, they took us, all the healthy ones, in brigades, hundred a group, hundred a group, they pushed us again in different lots, from there they put us on trucks and send us to the villages. It was cold. And they needed workers to collect the farm produce. So, they sent us on the field to collect potatoes, cucumbers, all kind of different produce. There I worked a couple weeks, we got food, we got rest. Not good condition, at least you could bath our self, eat plenty potatoes, the farmers are giving us bread, give us milk and we worked.

David: Who's in charge of this camp?

Charlie: The Germans brought us in by daytime; they brought us into the farms. At night, they brought us in, in different housing. In different kind of housing, in the farm housing, in the, how you call it?

David: Barns?

Charlie: In the barns, and they watched us, the Germans.

David: Who was it? The SS?

Charlie: No, this other kind of unit, special unit. After a while, the season was over, and they took us to work in Stettin. In the port of Stettin. There we were working for, from that day they took us, from 1943 *(1944[84])* late fall, until 1945, beginning of the year. In port, I work about year and a half. We were loading and unloading ships for the Germany navy and every day, we went to work, the camp was outside

---

[83] Quick, quick, make it quick!

[84] Records indicate the Szaja Lelonek fought in the Warsaw Uprising, September 1944.

of town, we went in cars, railroad cars. And at night, we came back to the camp. All day we worked, all kinds of work. We were loading and unloading and the Americans were bombing or the English were bombing the towns. They took us with trains. They made us clean the streets. Of course, the bombing was very fierce. Every couple of days the Americans came and bombed. I saw, during the time, different people working in different camps. They call them the Pashakees, people wearing the stripe uniform, concentration people. People from concentration camp came, also to work in different project.

I like to mention that I, after the Germans took me prisoner, I changed my identity. My name is Shayah Lelonek. Only, how to make me sure that I should not forget my name, I change my name of Jelonek, instead Lelonek, which sound very gentile. And the name of Shayah was changed to Stanislaw. And with that documentation, I came with that name I came into the prison camp. And everyone called me Stanislaw. And to work in the camp and go out, in the port, in work everyone has to wear a number and a name. So I still have in my possession the name of Stanislaw Jelonek. With that documentation you have to show coming in, leaving, going to the toilet, leaving, hanging around on the premises, in the port. Because the Gestapo and SS was cruising around and watching, that no strangers should come in, or no subversive work should be done. So if they ask for a document, I have it. And my name was Stanislaw Jelonek. With that document, I came to the end, through to the end of the war. And it helped me very much, my survival. Because after the war, when I said to the guys that "I am Jewish," they, no one wanted to believe. Because I didn't spill, never the, I never spill the...how you call it?

David: The beans.

Charlie: The beans. I was always keeping myself a low… in playing a good Polish Catholic. Yes, going back to the situation in Stettin, we worked a very hard every day. We was going out in the morning, coming back at night. The life was more or less organized in the prison

54

camp. You have to be very active because the condition was very miserable. We was getting every week one loaf of bread, that weighed one pound. This has to be cut in seven pieces. Every day we ate a couple ounces of bread, by noontime, we was getting, half a bowl of soup, and it mean water with dirt, at night we came back from work, we get another half a bowl of soup, it mean dirt with water. In the morning, I ate a slice of bread, which was very thin… with water. And we organized sugar in the port with stealing. Every day we brought in a couple pieces of sugar, or sugar in pieces, or sugar in (?), in the pockets. Whoever was healthy and willing to live, belong to the organization. That mean, whenever we could, we was stealing from the ship, like sardines, pieces of meat, fish, sugar, pieces of sugar, potatoes, vegetables. Whoever didn't belong to the organization, meaning he was not active in the units of the prison camp, these people starved and died. I was a very active member in the prison. I was on the committee, we helped organize expeditions, to organize food, we always was very successful. And even though the condition was so bad, imagine, how can you live on a pound of bread a week and a couple quart of water? We have food for us, not plentiful and we shared with these most, most unfortunate people which were lazy or you couldn't, they couldn't overcome the troubles. And they were not able to go and get things, we shared, wherever was possible. The hunger was so big in the camp, that when you was eating bread and a crumb would fell down on the floor, another guy was standing on the side, went down with his lips, and picked up that piece of bread, the crumb from the floor, that it shouldn't get lost. Plenty guys, I mean Polish citizens were shot, killed for trying to go out and grab a couple of potatoes, for get a couple pieces of carrots, or vegetables.

We were so brave, that from camp, we change in civilian clothing and we ventured out to the town to buy food. I was assigned one day to go out and to buy food in the town, which was a couple blocks away and I was apprehended by a German policeman. He took me on the side, he searched me. He found on me 22 marks, German marks. He took away the money from me and beat me up a little. And he said if he will see me again, he will give me to the Gestapo. This was an old German policeman. And he didn't know I that I'm Jewish. Otherwise, ha! He will bring me to the Gestapo for sure. I went back to the camp.

How we walked out from the camp? It is interesting, we were, we bribed the guards, which were older Germans, and we told them that they should look the other side, something is going on, some people fighting. We cut through, up, we have special scissors, we cut through wire near the floor, and we crawl through the wire fence on the other side and then we hooked up again, with thin wire the opening. And in that place, people are coming and going, in and out. Whenever it be decided a man has to go get food, to acquire food, it was a decision. And when the line came on me, I could not refuse and I went gladly. A couple of times I went and I bought fish, carrots, and potatoes. And it was successful. Only the last time when I got caught, I got scared. And I said to mine organization, to the other friends, that maybe that same policeman will watch me and try to catch me. Because I was go, I committed a crime. I went through, I went out from the camp without permission. Secondly, I was wearing, I got myself clothing, civilian clothing, which we obtained. We wore special uniform with a mark, Cris K. G., Cris Kapagania black uniforms. And there I wore a civilian suit. And he said, so if the Gestapo will get me, they will see me in civilian clothes, they will shot me. And it was true. I could get shot on the spot. I decide because I was a suspect already, that guy will maybe watch for me. Because he was in that district a cop. And I didn't go anymore. I have other assignments in different times. I went out at night. About a mile away was a farm and there were potatoes, digged in and covered up in the sand for the winter. So we was opening the trenches and was stealing the potatoes. Everyone was carrying, 20, 30, 40 pounds in bags. We brought them back to the camp, and hid them away and so in such a way we were have, we prepared food. Other guys went out and was stealing vegetables. We cooked food. Where we have at night... because it was there was a kitchen, some place in the camp. So we were cooking food; potatoes, vegetables. And whoever was willing to bring in food, these people got food. And the leftovers we shared with all the people who couldn't get food. And such a way we always, the willing and the better organized people, were trying to get food and always got something or potatoes, or vegetables, anything that was nourishing.

It was a big help. In such condition, when a pound of bread was lasting a week. At least we have a couple of potatoes or a couple pieces vegetables cooked and heated, it was a big help. Now the situation was going on, for a year and a half, we worked, they took us out sometimes from Stettin and they brought us into Bering, they brought us in different cities where the Americans bombed. And they was bringing us steady back to the camp. There, finally came the situation that the Russians broke through the fronts. And they were moving closer to Germany. So when the Russian armies were moving and pushing the Germans to their own country, we saw that the war is coming closer to us again. One day in 1944 before Christmas, they said that we packing and moving. They took the whole camp and told us we marching west, that is, that is because we were in Stettin and said we marching toward Hamburg.

David: So, it was the front?

Charlie: No.

David: No?

Charlie: They didn't want to deliver us to the Russians. They was pushing us to the west. We didn't know the difference where we was. No difference where we was going. So leaving Stettin, we were very disappointed. More or less we have conditions, which were possible to survive. Except the bombardments which from the Americans and the English, it was more or less possible with the help of the organization to get some food, the work was done in the port, and it wasn't too annoying. And the guards were not pushing us so hard. So we hoped that even with the worst conditions, if they let us stay until the end, we could survive, most of us. Whoever die from hunger, die from hunger.

When we….and only, no one was harmed in such a way. That is, no one was poisoning us. Only we was praying that we should stay until the end. Only when we started to move, we saw new trouble. Because we knew already that, in that conditions, marching to nowhere, a lot of us will be the victims. After marching a couple days, we stopped. We were without food, without water, they pushed us in, in these kinds of barns, it was cold and then they said, the Germans, they would destroy us if we did not follow them. The conditions got more dangerous. The guards told us we should keep move to the west. Only, it was impossible, practical, move on the roads. Because the army was moving on the roads. And we saw a lot of activity. For us, there was no place where to move. They was moving us at night.

Finally, we arrived to the town of Rinne, which is in the North Sea, where they put us on an island and there they organized a new camp. *(On Charlie's ITS inquiry card it is documented that he arrived in Schraprode Kr. the Bergen Island in 1944,[85] an island in the Baltic Sea. It is 183 km/114 miles from Stettin.)* This was January 1945. There the Germans was building different kinds of project. Until now, until lately, I found out, much after the war, many, many years, that from Brown, the guy which was giving the Americans how… the way how to make missiles, there they was working on the project, how to launch missiles and from there they was launching missiles, the V1 and V2 which was destroying the English cities. There we work very hard in cement work. Other works we were making different silos for these, how you call them? For launching these missiles. The work was very, very hard one. The conditions were very miserable. A lot of guys died hunger and from hard work. I survived that too. In that, in that camp, we was working January, February, March. In April the work almost stopped, we saw that something bad is going on. The German, it was an island, we saw the German ships moving back and forth, we saw different SS units moving away, coming up, going away. And they left us without work, without food. We were on our own. We were very much concerned.

---

[85] ITS inquiry card (31408151-0-1). Courtesy of USHMM.

Because on our own, we saw that they could destroy us. Because, not giving us the food, we have nothing to eat. And it was a question of survival. Whatever we have to eat, we have to steal. If they catch us stealing, they will shot us. Finally came the month of May *(May 8, 1945, in Schraprode Kr. Bergen Island [86])*, and the Russians landed on the island and they told us to go home.

---

[86] ITS inquiry card (31408151-0-1). Courtesy of USHMM.

CHAPTER 10

WHY ARE YOU ALIVE?

Charlie: Where was our home? We didn't know ourselves. The biggest achievement was in that time when the Russians freed us and said the war is over. They gave every guy 2 pounds of bread, 2 loaves of bread, a pound each. We was marching around with the loafs of bread like having treasures. After a couple of days, we left the camp and was heading toward town. I arrived back in Stettin *(183 km/114 miles)* and there I was tried...was trying to go back to Poland. It took me very long time until I reach the train. The trains were destroyed, bridges were bombard. I went through hell until I reached Poland. I came back to Warsaw *(599 km/372 miles)*. I came back to Warsaw and I saw very few Jewish people, practical nobody. The town was mostly destroyed. The leftovers were ugly looking. The people in Warsaw was trying to get back to their normal life without Jewish people. I decided to go back to my hometown Sierpc *(127 km/77 miles)*. I went to train and bought a ticket, destination Sierpc. I came down after a couple hours on the train and I arrived at Sierpc in the station. From the station to the town is about 2 kilometer. I walked down with a rucksack and no one recognized me. No one knew who I am. Right, in the town, near the little square, little park, which is in the section of the town, a guy my age, a Polack, recognize me. He said to me: "Lelonek, this you?

You are still alive?" And I said to him: "Yes, I am still alive." *(He said:)* "Get killed?" *(I said:)* "What you think, that everyone is dead?" "Yes," he said: "every Jew is dead, why you are alive?" After such a welcome I felt very bad. I came down to town and I went down to city hall, and I presented mine, myself and I said: "I am a Lelonek, the son of Yitzchak Mayer Lelonek, and I am requesting contact with Jewish people." "Oh!" they said: "There is a few. In a house, not far from here, there are living a couple of Jewish people." And they gave me the address.

I came into that house, and I said: "I am Lelonek" and no one wanted to believe me. They said: "Lelonek who? What's your name?" I said: "Shayah." They looked at me and they said: "What? Shayah Lelonek. You are not Lelonek." I said: "You may believe me. You want to talk to in Yiddish?" I said: "Yeah, I want to talk in Yiddish." So I introduced myself, and no one recognized me. In there was Boris Niemoff,[87] Abraham Roberto and a couple other people from the towns around. There, they washed me, they shaved me, they gave me clothing and they said: "Yes, it is true, you are Shayah Lelonek." I was so black, changed. And it was impossible to recognize me.

Imagine, from the town of 6,000 Jewish people, were there, four people from Sierpc, two people from Biezun and one people, person from Zuromin. This was the leftover of the town. The situation wasn't much a happy one. First of all, the security of the Jewish people right after the war was very dangerous. The Polacks feared that maybe more Jewish people will come back. They attacked at night the Jewish home and destroyed, the Jewish people, which were coming home from the camps. In the town of Raciaz, 25 to 30 kilometers from Sierpc, 4 people came home. The Polish Archa or underworld, whatever you call them, attacked at night and killed them all, shot them, all four. We were very fearful, what should happen to us. We went to authorities and told them that the situation is not friendly. Everyone looking on

---

[87] Boris Niemoff's testimony, Shoah Foundation,
http://vhaonline.usc.edu/viewingPage.aspx?testimonyID=22544&returnIndex=0

us like we are outcasts, we are not welcome. They said, they can do nothing. Only they gave us, to everyone a machine gun. We were sleeping in the house with guns and machine guns. This was our protection. The door to the, to the...the doors from the house were barricaded for the night and what kind of life is that? When you have to sleep with a gun or machine gun, the doors barricaded and you are not sure? So we decided to move away from Sierpc.

David: Dad, what did you do during the day? Did you ever go back to your house?

Charlie: I went back, I went back to the Yiddisha gas,[88] where they called it the Jewish section, the most of the Jewish section was erased. The old houses were destroyed or burnt out. And the people, the population told us, the Germans were looking for treasures in the Jewish homes. They erased every house. Of course, people were hiding everything, they found all kinds of treasurers. The inner city was survived, the house, which I was living, it was a brick house, survived. And I never went in there, because I was scared, maybe the people would not like me.

David: Were there people in there?

Charlie: Yes. The house was occupied by Polacks. I stayed in Sierpc a couple weeks and then we decided we have to move away from Sierpc to go to bigger city with there is more concentration of Jewish people. From there, we moved away to Watch, where we met other people, from there we started our way back to Germany. *(1079 km/670 miles from Sierpc to Lampertheim, Germany.[89])* Which, we were there until we came to the United States. Okay.

---

[88] Jewish section

[89] AEF (Allied Expeditionary Forces) Assembly Registration Card, #304295, 12/13/1945, Szaja Lelonek (b. 5/20/1914), assigned to DP Centre 578 Lampertheim. To USA on 4/30/1949. International Tracing Service courtesy of USHMM.

(On August 23, 1946 Charlie wrote a letter while living in the Lampertheim displaced persons camp to the Sierpc Relief Committee in New York about what happened in postwar Sierpc: [90]

I was also in our Sierpc a few months. It was difficult to endure that. All the houses are still standing, but without Jews. It appears sorrowful - there are no Jews with their payos, [91] nor our youth who used to promenade in the market and on Plodiker St. There is a general fright for only the thought that here lived your acquaintances and near ones and a fear overcomes you - the cemetery plowed under, the trees chopped down, there is no longer a remainder. One can no longer remain there *(in Sierpc);* I have left everything and came over here. I live here in a UNRRA camp.

On March 16, 1947 Charlie wrote another letter to the Sierpc Relief Committee about postwar Sierpc:

I can with deep, difficulty, share with you an episode that was related to me by survivors about the lives and demise of my uncle, Shlomo Lelonek's, children. My uncle's children were away to Warsaw in 1939. There they lived a difficult war life. Their son-in-law, Shaul Widorowitz, born in Raciaz, helped them with everything after the liquidation in the year 1943 of the Warsaw ghetto. Shaul Widorowitz hid the entire family in a bunker. In the year 1944 they were captured through Poles and were turned over to the German Gestapo. Manya Lelonek, Boruch Lelonek, and the

---

[90] Letters from Icek, Hersz, Shayah and Moshe Lelonek, Yaakov Hutnik and David Lazinsky from Lampertheim to the Sierpcer Relief Committee in NY. Courtesy of YIVO Institute. See Part V of the book.
[91] Sideburns or side locks.

young Chaim were shot immediately, and Rochel Widorowitz with her daughter, a six-year old girl, and her husband, Shaul Widorowitz were brought to "Powiac," that is a Warsaw prison. From there, Rochel and her young daughter on one early morning were terminated and Shaul Widorowitz went away from the prison with a group of friends and hid themselves in a bunker. After great suffering and tortures, frightful endurance of hunger and thirst, they managed to remain alive until the great day of liberation of Warsaw by the "Red Army." They had lived until liberation in a cellar in a bombed-out house on a street where there was no longer any living human presence. Exhausted from the great tragedy and suffering, Shaul Widorowitz drags himself in the beginning of February 1945 to Sierpc. He was the first Jew to return to Sierpc. He went to his home in Dales St. by the baker Gradzicki and wanted to search there for anything *(remaining)* of his possessions. In the evening, ostensible military men from the security service entered the house and demanded that he establish his identity and took him away. And thus he went away from that moment and in a secretive manner perished through the murderous Polish hands.

I, coming to Sierpc from Germany in June 1945, tried everything to find some scent of his body, but all was without success.)

CHAPTER 11

LIFE IN RUSSIA

(Second recording session begins:)

David: Okay, all right. Dad, what happened to your family while you were in prison at the POW camp?

Charlie: Not exactly. I will start a little earlier.

David: Okay.

Charlie: When I volunteered and went to the army, my folks were sitting in some place in Russia, in a Soviet farm, collective. And then, while I volunteered to the army, the authorities permitted them to leave the collective farm and they moved into the village, to the town, whatever you call it. The town was the name Vatt and it was in Gorky reyon, region rather, in Gorky region. And from that time, since I left, they got some privileges to enjoy because I was serving in the army and I was defending in one way, mine own honor and the honor of the Soviet Union. Of course, the privileges weren't so great. It was a little better, like ordinary people, which have not children in the army. For example, they gave them a empty farmhouse, which was empty at a time ago. Of course, the people which were living there were not friendly to the Soviet government or they were, in a way, enemies, accordingly, to the local situation. And they, these people were resettled someplace, an unknown place where criminals or unfriendly citizens are resettled. The house they obtained it from the Soviet as a presentation for their friendliness, to the people which have children in the army. And the other members of the family, which were there, got the same privilege. They got the privileges of buying food and other commodities, which were necessary for the family. Like, when they got the ration, for bread, they gave a double ration. Which was very important wartime because all Russia was hungry. They got a plot, where they could raise a garden and plant vegetables and potatoes. The government supplied the all the necessary things which should make the thing grow, in the field or in garden; like a horse, a plow and all kinds of things. Which was needed. I will say that while I served in the army, the authorities were trying to be helpful to mine parents, to the family. The younger kids, which were not old, even to go to school, went to work and worked on the collective farms. Which they got paid in food and grain and bread and potatoes instead of money. Which was a big help in a very hungry time.

I was in steady contact with them, writing them letters. Of course, they were very not too happy. Only, my parents were aware that once you are in the war, war is not a happy situation. And they accepted the situation as it was. That all the men in the Soviet Union are fighting and I am between them, I am man too and I should fight to destroy the Nazi enemy.

When I was taken prisoner and this was in 1943 *(1944[92])*, the way I mentioned before, a day before Yom Kippur, I wrote them the same day a postcard from the front, that accordingly, "We are in very unfriendly territory, we not far from our home place *(Sierpc)*." I mentioned: "not far from our home place" because I could not mention, not explain the location where we are. "And there is a possibility that we will go soon on an action. And if everything will go

---

[92] Records indicate the Szaja Lelonek fought in the Warsaw Uprising, September 16, 1944, Rosh HaShanah eve.

the way we wanted, we will have a chance to step in mine town of Bird, as a free citizen, in a free country of Poland." This was my last postcard, which I sent to mine parents and from that on everything was lost. Of course, when I was taken prisoner I couldn't write. I mentioned before, I was taken away from the Polish land and they took us prisoner to Germany, where I work there for the war. My parents were all the time living in despair. And they got a notice from the Soviet authorities, that I went in action and they lost contact with me and there is a possibility that I am dead. *(Szaja Lelonek is listed as having died or went missing without a trace during the Warsaw Uprising, on September 22, 1944.*[93] [94] [95]*)* Anyway, the situation was unclear. After a couple of months, they got a notation, that "lost in action" and there is no trace of me. They would get, kind of compensation for life from the authorities because I was fighting on their side, they feel sorry and they send condolences to the parents. My father was very unhappy and brokenhearted, he was sitting shivah after me and he said Kaddish. Which is an unusual thing because there wasn't there a minyan[96] every day. And the family made up as a fact, de facto, that there was no me. Right after the war, when I was freed, I was trying to rectify the situation. It wasn't possible to send telegrams right after the war. So I sent a special letter by mail through the authorities that "I'm alive and I'm in Poland" and telling them that another letter will follow and I will assign a place where to find me and I dated the day of May 1945. Because, accordingly, so much mail was lost in the wartime, that people received letters from the war, from the 43, 44, when people were really dead 2, 3 years and the mail was still coming. When mine parents received that letter, they didn't want to believe. So, they went to the authorities, they showed them. They said: "Yes, it was mine handwriting and the date is after the war already. There is a possibility,"

---

[93] *Book of Buried Polish Soldiers Killed During World War II.* 1993, page 253.
[94] *Book of the Dead on the Field of Glory: Polish People's Army Soldiers who were Killed, Died of Wounds and Missing During the Second World War.* 1974. Page 874.
[95] *United Illustrated Encyclopedia of the Warsaw Uprising: List of Participants of the Warsaw Uprising Soldiers.* 2002. Page 797.
[96] Gathering of ten men and a quorum for Jewish public prayer.

they figured, "maybe someone is playing a trick." Only, after a couple of days later came another letter by mail and it verify that I am alive and in one piece and I am in Warsaw. If there will be a possibility in the near future, they will be able to see me again. I like to mention, while I recollect myself, when my mother received the news that I was lost in action, she lost her ability to move, she was lame. She was from the day on, until I sent a letter that I am alive, until that day she didn't move, it was for 2 and a half, 3 years. *(Charlie was off 1 year in his estimation since he recounted being captured in 1943 instead of 1944.[97])* As soon as she, we got the letter, that I am alive and I'm in one piece, she got up from bed and moved a couple steps. It was a real miracle. If her son is alive, she getting healthy again and from that moment on until her last day of life she walked. And all the time which they thought I am killed or lost, she couldn't walk. She was paralyzed.

---

[97] Records indicate the Szaja Lelonek fought in the Warsaw Uprising, Yom Kippur, 1944.

CHAPTER 12

FAMILY REUNION

Charlie: I tried to contact them in, from Warsaw and was trying to tell them they should leave and repatriate to Poland, where there is a possibility to meet each other. I refused, by myself to go back to Russia and meet them because I knew the situation, once you going in, you cannot go out. *(See Historical Context: Plight of the Soviet Jews* [98] [99]*)* So right away my parents were trying how to leave, to repatriate to Poland.

Historical Context: Plight of the Soviet Jews

At the conclusion of World War II, 3 million Jews were living in Soviet-occupied territories. The Soviet government did not prioritize the reunification of surviving family members. Refugees were forced to stay under Soviet dominion. All Soviets had their nationality listed on their ID cards. For Jewish Soviets, rather than their nationality, their ethnicity was listed as "Jewish." This ensured that they would be unable to assimilate into communist society as Stalin's goal was to eradicate diverse religious and cultural identities. Yet, their ability to study and practice Judaism was suppressed by the mandates of Soviet law. Though they may have wanted to be accepted as Soviets, they were viewed as outsiders, and at times of upheaval, they were used as scapegoats. Joseph Stalin, the dictator of the Soviet Union, persecuted Jewish intellectuals on

---

[98] Joseph Telushkin. *Jewish Literacy*. NY: William Morrow and Co., 1991
[99] Beckerman, Gal. *When They Come for Us, We'll Be Gone; The Epic Struggle to Save Soviet Jewry*. NY: Houghton Mifflin Harcourt, 2011.

fabricated charges in the "Doctors' Plot" and the "Night of Murdered Poets."

An international underground movement smuggled religious articles and books into the Soviet Union. Distribution and study of the materials were conducted in a clandestine manner and under the threat of arrest and banishment to Siberia. The covert nature of learning about and practicing Judaism restricted access to Jewish life to only a brave few. By 1965, only about 60 synagogues remained in the Soviet Union.

Israel's Six Day War sparked a new emotion in Soviet Jews. They felt enormous pride in the victory of the young Jewish state; while struggling with the Soviet military support being given to the Arab states. In 1970, nine Soviet Jews and two non-Jewish Soviets were arrested in a failed attempt to hijack an airline with the motive to bring world attention to the plight of Soviet Jewry. International media coverage of the hijacking and the mockery of a trial with disproportionate sentences gave the Soviet Jewry movement worldwide prominence.

Post World War II, American Jews struggled with their silence during the Holocaust and their own their identity as Jewish Americans in the era of the State of Israel. In the late 1950s, Holocaust survivors ended their painful silence and started publishing their accounts. Concomitantly, America's intelligence on the concentration camps and refusal to intercede was declassified. American Jewry had a deep sense of anger and guilt. The plight of Soviet Jews presented an opportunity for the Jewish world community to redeem itself. The protest movement on behalf of Soviet Jewry spread throughout the United States. In 1964, Jacob Birnbaum founded the Student Struggle for Soviet Jewry (SSSJ). College students from Yeshiva University, Jewish Theological Seminary, Queens College and Columbia attended the first SSSJ rally on May 1, 1964. Birnbaum used the civil rights movement as a blueprint to rally support and effect change for Soviet Jews. The SSSJ demanded the Jews' right to live as Jews within Russia and to emigrate if they wished. Rallies publicizing the oppression of Soviet Jews were held from New York to California. Other Soviet Jewry support groups sprung up around the United States. Many of them joined together to create the Union of Councils for Soviet Jewry led by Leo Rosenblum. The Jewish Defense League, headed by Meir Kahane, harassed Soviet diplomats stationed in the United States.

Historical Context Continued: Plight of the Soviet Jews

Initially, Soviet leadership made no concessions. Allowing Jews to emigrate would be a tacit admission that socialism was not for everyone. However, after the Six Day War, the spirit of Soviet Jewry was revived. Thousands of Soviet Jews began to study and practice Judaism and attended public Simchat Torah celebrations. The international unrest caused by the Soviet Jewish revival tipped the scales in favor of easing emigration. Many Soviet Jews applied for emigration visas to Israel. By the early 1970s, many were receiving permission. The Soviet Jewish intellectuals, though, were refused exit visas and became known as "Refusniks." They were no longer accepted by their state, lost their jobs yet were refused from leaving the country and restarting their lives elsewhere. The Soviet government often imprisoned them. They became the face and rallying cry for the Soviet's human rights abuses and a focal point in political negotiations.

Soviet Jewry groups lobbied in Washington. The recognition of the human rights abuses resulted in the congressionally sponsored Jackson-Vanik amendment. The amendment linked the Soviet Union's trade designation as a "Most Favored Nation Status" to freedom of emigration for Soviet Jews and the end of human rights violations. This was the first time human rights were tied to a trade treaty. The Soviets were enraged at the attempt to meddle in their domestic policies and choked off the emigration of Soviet Jews. Eventually, to attain trade benefits, the Soviets changed their emigration policies, allowing Jews to emigrate en masse. This significant shift in Soviet policy was a major factor in the demise of the Soviet Union. By the late 1980s, for the large majority of Soviet Jews, emigration was achievable. Refusniks and the 1970 airplane hijackers were freed from the Gulag and allowed to emigrate to Israel and America. By 1990, more than ten thousand Soviet Jews were leaving monthly. Eventually, 1.5 million Jewish Soviets emigrated, mostly to America and Israel.

Of course, and they, and they have a good excuse. They found a son and the authorities should help to get them united. And they very friendly for that type of thing. And they came back to Poland. And from Poland, they went back to Austria. I was in that time in Germany. I went down to Austria on the borderline and I met them. I took them over with me in Germany where I was camping, in the UN, UNRRA camp, where in Lampertheim, Germany where I was with a lot of friends. *(1079 km/670 miles from Sierpc, Poland to Lampertheim, Germany.*

See Historical Context: Displaced Persons Camp in Lampertheim, Germany [100]

[101] [102] [103] [104] [105]) I took them over there. I put them in an apartment, my sister, brothers, my parents, and I was trying to normalize their life. We should live more or less happily, as a family together for a while. Of course, I by myself made up my mind not to stay in Germany. Because I was single, I have all kind of ideas for the future, and I didn't like the life in Germany. First of all, the income where we were living was not a nice one, there was no black market business. Secondly, this not a way of conducting myself, being alive, you have to be a productive man. In Germany, we were all more or less living normal. Only, we were like put together in a ghetto. The camps were like an open ghetto. People were coming and going; only it wasn't a way of living. In all the days, which were doing nothing, we did a little social life, we were meeting with people. And we were trying to tie up all our social life a little bit. Like we were trying to organize a Chalutz, Zionists activities, Jewish National Fund activities and so on. People even were try to learn trades which they figured they will use in the future. And more or less, the activities were primarily directed for the near future when people will start to live a more productive life, not sitting around doing nothing. In that time, we saw different people from American organizations coming down and trying to organize us, teaching us, to rehabilitate us, to help us think differently. After that gruesome and

---

[100] http://www.ushmm.org/museum/exhibit/online/dp/camp9.htm

[101] http://dpcamps.ort.org/camps/germany/us-zone/us-zone-vi/lampertheim/

[102] AEF (Allied Expeditionary Forces) Assembly Registration Card, #304295, 12/13/1945, Szaja Lelonek (b. 5/20/1914), assigned to DP Centre 578 Lampertheim. To USA on 4/30/1949. International Tracing Service courtesy of USHMM.

[103] Szaja Lelonek is listed on the displaced persons camp at Lampertheim census September 29, 1946, page 22. International Tracing Service, courtesy of USHMM.

[104] Pesa Kadecki's sister, Rachel married Moshe Hersz Wolman, their oldest son was Abram Wolman, who emigrated to America on October 26, 1922, and was sponsored by his uncle William Kadetsky.

[105] Icek and Pesa Lelonek and Hersz Lelonek's "Application for Assistance." "Care and Maintenance" files were created in Germany and were submitted to the International Refugee Organization (IRO) so families would qualify as displaced persons (DP) eligible for assistance or emigration. International Tracing Service courtesy of USHMM.

terrible years of the war. It was a big confusion. People didn't know what to do with themselves. Where to go, what to do? The most people lost hope in humanity; they saw too many bad things. Other people were disoriented, they say it doesn't pay to do anything, the life is no good, the world is cruel. They were sit. They were sitting doing nothing with apathy.

Historical Context: Displaced Persons Camp in Lampertheim, Germany

Lampertheim was a small Jewish displaced persons camp that opened on December 15, 1945, primarily to give more space for refugees from the overcrowded Zeilsheim Displaced persons camp. Situated between Mannheim and Darmstadt in the Frankfurt district of the American zone of occupation, Lampertheim boasted a library of about 500 Yiddish, German, and Hebrew books, all of which were donated by American Jewish organizations and the Jewish Agency in Palestine. Lampertheim also maintained a secular elementary school, a Talmud Torah (religious elementary school), a kindergarten, a synagogue, a kosher kitchen, a theater group and a small orchestra. In December 1947, religious residents of the camp protested against a theater performance on the Sabbath. The camp's newspaper was entitled Frayhayt (Freedom) and was printed until May 24, 1949, when Lampertheim closed. At its peak in 1946-47, the camp housed over 1,200 DPs. They lived in requisitioned private houses in the village. The camp organized its own civic administration, with thirty unarmed policemen and uniformed fire service. There was a post office which operated as a tracing bureau for missing relatives of the camp's community. The health center in the camp was operated by doctors, who were at the same time DPs and residents of the center. A summer camp was organized for the children. A few kilometers from the town, the camp operated a kibbutz for thirty young people training in farming in preparation for their emigration to Palestine.[100][101]

Szaja (Charlie) Lelonek registered as a displaced person under the auspices of the Allied Expeditionary Forces on December 13, 1945, and was placed in the Displaced persons camp in Lampertheim.[102][103] He lists Abraham Wolman, a maternal Kadetsky first cousin, as a family contact in America.[104] Yitzchak Mayer and Pesa Lelonek arrived in Lodz, Poland on June 6, 1946, and were reunited with Charlie on September 6, 1946. Hersz (Tzvi) Lelonek registered in Lampertheim on August, 1946.[105] The Lelonek, Lazinsky and Hutnik families lived at Lampertheim-Hessen 16, UNRRA Area 1021, Ludwig 21, US Zone Germany. On February 18, 1947, Miriam Lelonek married Yaacov Hutnik in Lampertheim. From 1946-1949, the family wrote 33 letters to the "Sierpcer Relief Committee" in Brooklyn, New York.

Historical Context Continued: Displaced Persons Camp in Lampertheim, Germany

Moshe Lelonek described his activities in the Lampertheim Displaced persons camp in his "roots work."

> In 1946, we came to Germany and stayed there until 1948. We stayed in the group of Jews who were Holocaust survivors. In this town *(Lampertheim)*, I was among those who set up a Hebrew school and I ran it. The students were ages 5 to 15, they were studying for the first time in their lives, because before then, they were in concentration camps. In addition, I volunteered for a committee that welcomed people who wanted to fight and serve the IDF for Israel's War of Independence. At the end of 1948, we went to Marseille. We were there for a number of months waiting for winter to pass, so we can go on a ship to go up to the land *(of Israel)*. In early 1949, we boarded the ship, "Marathon" and within a week we got to the state of Israel.

Charlie was involved in activities to preserve the memory and history of the Sierpc community. He participated in a first annual Yizkor gathering on November 8, 1947, in Germany, commemorating the day the Jews of Sierpc were exiled and the 5,000 members of the community who were murdered by the Nazis. He attended another Yizkor gathering on March 20, 1949. In 1948, the book, *Zaml Book Fun Sierpcer Shairit HaChurban* was published by the Sierpcer Jewish Committee (US Zone Germany). S. Lelonek is listed as one of five people on the book's Coordinator Committee. From the preface:

> Two years have already gone by after the terrible events of the war. We, the survivors of Sierpc, in an effort to commemorate the town in which we were born and where we lived until Hitler wrought havoc, have decided to give a written account of all those events. Immediately after the war there was no possibility to have this book printed because we did not yet know of each other and because we were not in a position to put down our thoughts. After life slowly resumed its normal path, we formed a committee in charge of mutual assistance and of establishing a permanent connection among the members. It is our aim to create a book on all those events that happened during the war.

> This book is meant to be a monument commemorating all those beloved persons that died or were killed in action as heroes. -The Editors."

CHAPTER 13

HOME: AMERICA AND ISRAEL

Charlie: One day, I met the representative of the Jewish Organization, UNRRA, United Jewish Appeal people, they came down and was talking to us and they ask us if we are interested to change our system of life and they called a meeting and I went there and we discussed broader, there is a possibility now to emigrate to the US if someone wanted. *(See Historical Context: United States Policy Towards Jewish Refugees, 1941–1952[106])* Other people came around and were advocating that there is possibility to go to Israel if we wanted. The Israeli delegations, which we call them the Berihah, they took a different approach. They said they will take the people from Germany bring them to Italy, put them on ships and bring them illegal into Israel. The American representatives with the UNRRA, registered and put up a list of names. So, on that time, I registered myself with one of UNRRA representatives and the UJA representatives. And they said, "Well, this is the first step for rehabilitation. We will bring that to the American authorities and we will present them your names. And if they will look in, in that, they will accept that there is no quota and refugees now

---

[106] Reprinted with permission from the US Holocaust Memorial Museum. "United States Policy Towards Jewish Refugees, 1941–1952." Holocaust Encyclopedia http://www.ushmm.org/wlc/en/article.php?ModuleId=10007094

right after the war, there is a possibility that the people which is getting registered will be going pretty soon to America." After a couple of months, I got a notice from the American General Consulate from Frankfurt in Germany, that they want to see me. I came over to them and they were talking to me, they asked me all kinds of questions, about my family, my status and they asked me if I want to go to the States? I said "Yes." They said "Okay, accepted," swore me in. They said, "Go home, where you are and wait for a telegram, they send you a date, that you should arrive to Blame Radin, from there you will go to the United States." After couple months again, I got a telegram and I arrived, I went to Blame Radin, and from they took me to the States.

This way, I came in, in the States without any difficulties, without any bothering, without any pushing and other guys came the same way, with the same position, they said, "If I will like America, I will stay. If I will not like being in America, I will go back. I will go to Israel." It was like a free choice, like going from here to Long Island or from here to Manhattan. We went to America for a job. We said, "look around, if we like it, we will stay, and if we will dislike it, we will go back. We changed our way go to a different direction." This way I came to America for a job. I came down and I looked around and saw life is normal here. There is all kind of possibilities, so I resettled, changed life, get organized and lead a normal life. And I settled in New York. From there I started to catch up, I learned a trade in lady's garments. I have a lot of friends which help me. People for my town, they teached me, they advised me, they gave me information; what to do, how to behave. And mine family was very helpful which I have in America. I met people, I started to have a normal life, started to socialize. I met an American girl, got married to her. Reorganize a life, have a family and we are living a normal life today.

Shalom.

Historical Context: United States Policy Towards Jewish Refugees, 1941-1952

Although thousands of Jews had been admitted into the United States under the combined German-Austrian quota from 1938-1941, the US did not pursue an organized and specific rescue policy for Jewish victims of Nazi Germany until early 1944.

While some American activists sincerely intended to assist refugees, serious obstacles to any relaxation of US immigration quotas included public opposition to immigration during a time of economic depression, xenophobia, and anti-Semitic feelings in both the general public and among some key government officials. Once the United States entered World War II, the State Department practiced stricter immigration policies out of fear that refugees could be blackmailed into working as agents for Germany.

It was not until January 1944 that President Franklin D. Roosevelt, under pressure from officials in his own government and an American Jewish community then fully aware of the extent of mass murder, took action to rescue European Jews. Following discussions with Treasury Department officials, he established the War Refugee Board (WRB) to facilitate the rescue of imperiled refugees. With the assistance of the American Jewish Joint Distribution Committee and the World Jewish Congress, as well as resistance organizations in German-occupied Europe, the WRB helped to rescue many thousands of Jews in Hungary, Romania, and elsewhere in Europe.

In April 1944, Roosevelt also directed that Fort Ontario, New York, become a free port for refugees. However, only a few thousand refugees were allowed there and they were from liberated areas, not from Nazi-occupied areas. They were in no imminent danger of deportation to killing centers in German-occupied Poland. Ultimately, Allied victory brought an end to Nazi terror in Europe and to the war in the Pacific. However, liberated Jews, suffering from illness and exhaustion, emerged from concentration camps and hiding places to discover a world which had no place for them. Bereft of home and family and reluctant to return to their prewar homelands, these Jewish displaced persons (DPs) were joined in a matter of months by more than 150,000 other Jews fleeing fierce anti-Semitism in Poland, Hungary, Romania, and the Soviet Union.

Most sought to begin a new life outside Europe. Palestine was the most favored destination of Jewish Holocaust survivors, followed by the United States. Immigration restrictions were still in effect in the United States after the war, and legislation to expedite the admission of Jewish DPs was slow in coming.

Historical Context Continued: United States Policy Towards Jewish Refugees, 1941-1952

President Harry S. Truman favored a liberal immigration policy toward DPs. Faced with congressional inaction, he issued an executive order, the "Truman Directive," on December 22, 1945. The directive required that existing immigration quotas be designated for displaced persons. While overall immigration into the United States did not increase, more DPs were admitted than before. About 22,950 DPs, of whom two-thirds were Jewish, entered the United States between December 22, 1945, and 1947 under provisions of the Truman Directive.

Congressional action was needed before existing immigration quotas could be increased. In 1948, following intense lobbying by the American Jewish community, Congress passed legislation to admit 400,000 DPs to the United States. Nearly 80,000 of these, or about 20 percent, were Jewish DPs. The rest were Christians from Eastern Europe and the Baltics, many of whom had been forced laborers in Germany. The entry requirements favored agricultural laborers to such an extent, however, that President Truman called the law "flagrantly discriminatory against Jews." Congress amended the law in 1950, but by that time most of the Jewish DPs in Europe had gone to the newly established state of Israel (founded on May 14, 1948).

By 1952, 137,450 Jewish refugees (including close to 100,000 DPs) had settled in the United States. The amended 1948 law was a turning point in American immigration policy and established a precedent for later refugee crises.

(Third recording session begins presumably after David has asked a question that was not recorded, whether Charlie ever saw people from concentrations camps:)

Charlie: When we were boarding, going to work, I got in to see the concentration camp people marching to work in a different direction to our train. And the situation are very gruesome. They was pushed around by SS guards and dogs. They was pushing them very hard to move very fast. It was very cold that day. No other days I met, the same group again it seems. The people wore no coats, they wore little stripped jackets, little striped pants and some wooden shoes. The noise was tremendous. And the guards were hollering, pushing them. And the animal's boxcars. Whoever didn't walk fast, they we're beating him terrible. I saw the same people; I think they were from Stutthof,[107] a concentration which was around Stettin. And this, that scene made a very bad impression on the war prisoners and all that people which were with me.

(Fourth recording session begins:)

David: (?) went to Israel?

Charlie: I left for America, I left the family behind. And I was in contact with them. The Israeli Berihah, so called, which was an underground organization, and they organized the refugees the leftovers from the war to go to Israel, was working intensively in the refugee camps. And they was trying to bring as a many people as possible to Israel. *(See Historical Context: Postwar Refugee Crisis and the Establishment of the State of Israel [108])* While I was in America, the State of Israel was declared as a free country. And the Israeli government together with their officers abroad was trying in the hardest way to bring in, the fastest way, many, many people which will secure the majority in militarily, in all the other ways around, strengthen the position of Israel, having a lot of people, the country will get stronger, the economy will get stronger and the people will populate it, it will be a blessing. My, my family decided this is the right opportunity. They registered in, in, to go to Israel.[109] [110] And with the help, with the Jewish,

---

[107] Stutthof Concentration Camp,
http://www.ushmm.org/wlc/en/article.php?ModuleId=10005197
[108] Reprinted with permission from US Holocaust Memorial Museum. "Postwar Refugee Crisis and the Establishment of the State of Israel." Holocaust Encyclopedia http://www.ushmm.org/wlc/en/article.php?ModuleId=10005459
[109] Icek, Pesa and Hersz Lelonek's "Care and Maintenance; Application for Assistance." They declare their intention to move to Israel: 2/24/1948 (America is crossed out). They listed their daughter, Tova Steiner, in Haifa, Newe Shannan as their contact person in Israel. International Tracing Service courtesy of USHMM.
[110] Miriam and Yaakov Lelonek's "Care and Maintenance; Application for Assistance." They declare intention to move to Israel: 1/6/1948. They list their contact as Miriam's brother in law, Abraham Steiner. International Tracing Service courtesy of USHMM.

Historical Context: Postwar Refugee Crisis and the Establishment of the State of Israel

During World War II, the Nazis deported between 7 and 9 million Europeans, mostly to Germany as slave labor. Within months of Germany's surrender in May 1945, the Allies repatriated to their home countries more than six million displaced persons (DPs; wartime refugees). Between 1.5 million and two million DPs refused repatriation.

Most Jewish survivors, who had survived concentration camps or had been in hiding, were unable or unwilling to return to Eastern Europe because of postwar anti-Semitism and the destruction of their communities during the Holocaust. Many of those who did return feared for their lives. In Poland, for example, locals initiated several violent pogroms. The worst was the one in Kielce in 1946 in which 42 Jews, all survivors of the Holocaust, were killed. These pogroms led to a significant second movement of Jewish refugees from Poland to the west.

Many Holocaust survivors moved westward to territories liberated by the western Allies. They were housed in displaced persons camps and urban displaced persons centers. The Allies established such camps in Allied-occupied Germany, Austria, and Italy for refugees waiting to leave Europe. Most of the Jewish displaced persons were in the British occupation zone in northern Germany and in the American occupation zone in the south. The British established a large displaced persons camp adjacent to the former concentration camp of Bergen-Belsen in Germany. Several large camps holding 4,000 to 6,000 displaced persons each - Feldafing, Landsberg, and Foehrenwald - were located in the American zone.

At its peak in 1947, the Jewish displaced person population reached approximately 250,000. While the United Nations Relief and Rehabilitation Administration (UNRRA) administered all of the displaced persons camps and centers, Jewish displaced persons achieved a large measure of internal autonomy.

A variety of Jewish agencies were active in the displaced persons camps. The American Jewish Joint Distribution Committee provided refugees with food and clothing, and the Organization for Rehabilitation through Training (ORT) offered vocational training. Jewish displaced persons also formed self-governing organizations, and many worked toward the establishment of a Jewish state in Palestine. There were central committees of Jewish displaced persons in the American and British zones, which, as their primary goals, pressed for greater immigration opportunities, and the creation of a Jewish homeland in Palestine.

Historical Context Continued: Postwar Refugee Crisis and the Establishment of the State of Israel

In the United States, immigration restrictions strictly limited the number of refugees permitted to enter the country. The British, who had received a mandate from the League of Nations to administer Palestine, severely restricted Jewish immigration there largely because of Arab objections. Many countries closed their borders to immigration. Despite these obstacles, many Jewish displaced persons attempted to leave Europe as soon as possible.

The Jewish Brigade Group, formed as a unit within the British army in late 1944, worked with former partisans to help organize the Brihah (literally "escape"), the exodus of 250,000 Jewish refugees across closed borders from inside Europe to the coast in an attempt to sail for Palestine. The Mosad le-Aliyah Bet, an agency established by the Jewish leadership in Palestine, organized "illegal" immigration (Aliyah Bet) by ship. However, the British intercepted most of the ships.

In 1947, for example, the British stopped the *Exodus 1947* at the port of Haifa. The ship had 4,500 Holocaust survivors on board, who were returned to Germany on British vessels. In most cases, the British detained the refugees, over 50,000, in detention camps on the island of Cyprus in the eastern Mediterranean Sea. The British use of detention camps as a deterrent failed, and the flood of immigrants attempting entry into Palestine continued. The internment of Jewish refugees, many of them Holocaust survivors, turned world opinion against British policy in Palestine. The report of the Anglo-American Commission of Inquiry in January 1946 led US president Harry Truman to pressure Britain into admitting 100,000 Jewish refugees into Palestine. As the crisis escalated, the British government decided to submit the problem of Palestine to the United Nations (UN). In a special session, the UN General Assembly voted on November 29, 1947, to partition Palestine into two new states, one Jewish and the other Arab, a recommendation that Jewish leaders accepted and the Arabs rejected.

After the British began the withdrawal of their military forces from Palestine in early April 1948, Zionist leaders moved to establish a modern Jewish state. On May 14, 1948, David Ben-Gurion, the chairman of the Jewish Agency for Palestine, announced the formation of the state of Israel, declaring, "The Nazi Holocaust, which engulfed millions of Jews in Europe, proved anew the urgency of the reestablishment of the Jewish State, which would solve the problem of Jewish homelessness by opening the gates to all Jews and lifting the Jewish people to equality in the family of nations."

the Israeli organization, they took the whole family at once and they brought them in *(January[111])* 1949 to Israel and they put them in Haifa. They settled in Haifa, they got work. I help them from the States to get some money, they should get an apartment or a condominium, they calling in that times. My father was old enough, he couldn't work anymore. All the other members of the family took jobs. They settled in different apartments, they are happily today, living in Israel. Mine parents were living from 1949-1973 *(1967)*, until that war year.[112] The year they were living happily. When the war broke out in Israel, my father got sick and he died *(May 31, 1967)*. And my mother died a month later *(June 24, 1967)*. Being left alone, she succumbed and died too. So, both people died in Israel. And they died a normal death. They buried in Haifa. I visited them a couple times. Even if death is a very sad situation, it's the end of life. Anyway, I am happy and proud that I could see my parents die in a normal way. Not to be destroyed by enemies, the people. I can come there. I can put up my thoughts, even cry a minute and see the graves and the names written forever in Israel.

(Fifth recording session begins:)

David: While you were in the camp, were people killed? And by when? And how? and whom?

Charlie: Not exactly. People were not killed. Because most of the war prisoners, which I were between them, were Poles, Polacks. And the neighboring camps around us, which were plenty of war prisoners, were Russians, which were mistreated and not destroyed. There were Yugoslavs, Italians, English people, which was in the same compound was an American camp. So the situation was not so miserable. It was bad. We really didn't see killings because there was no Jews to kill there. The most of the people, which were, there were other nationalities,

---

111 Ester Yagoda on August 27, 2010. Bluma Lazinsky told me that they left via the port of Trieste, Italy on the Atzmaut.
112 Six Day War, June 5-10, 1967.
http://www.britannica.com/EBchecked/topic/850855/Six-Day-War See background and summary of events leading to war.

except Jews. So it was plenty suffering, people died from hunger, people died from disease. Only I didn't witness any killing with a gun, or with a rifle, or with a pistol, someone should be put down right on the spot. I assume if there will be Jews, there will be a lot of killings, every minute. Only, it seems to me that every other nationality were treated much better and not so harsh like they treated the Jewish people. Thank you.

(Sixth recording session begins:)

David: Dad, were you ever hurt, wounded or in bad health during the war?

Charlie: Yes, I was wounded twice in action. I have still marks in my finger, in my shoulder. I think a piece of shrapnel is lodged in my shoulder and will stay until the end of my life. I got a piece of shrapnel in my small...

David: Right hand.

Charlie: Right. My hand. My finger on my hand is crooked. And which of course will stay that way. I am not suffering especially badly. In winter, it hurts me a little. I was, I got sick in the field in action. I had malaria. They took me away with a big temperature. I woke up 6 to 8 weeks later in a hospital. I was unconscious about 6 to 8 weeks. I suffered very much, I lost weight, and I recovered after being in the hospital a couple times. I learned how to behave. I manipulate to stay a little longer. That didn't help me. After I recuperate, I came back to my strength, they send again in action. This was going on with everyman in the wartime. After you recuperated, you refreshed yourself, you rested, they send us again back on the front.

David: Were you ever sick in the prisoner camp?

Charlie: In prison camp, yes I got sick too and it was a very, very grave situation. In 1944, in fall, close to Christmas time I got a cold, high temperature. Of course the situation was very miserable. We haven't got nourishment. We got very little food. And to get sick, it was the end almost. Accordingly, everyone has to move out from the barracks and go to work. Only, I couldn't lift myself, I have a 103 temperature. And my head was bouncing and I lost power. I couldn't stand up. So the German authorities took me to a doctor and the doctor diagnosed that maybe it's pneumonia or something else, they put me in an ambulance, I took a chance and they took me to the hospital for a checkup. There they checked me up thoroughly and they gave me a document, which is still in my possession that everything is negative. I just have a bad cold. And they send me back to the barracks. And gave me a chance to rest 3 days. And after that, I should go back to work. Looking on that situation today, I wonder from where I took so much courage, to go with an ambulance to a hospital checkup, knowing that they will check me through. Anyway, I was lucky enough, and I went through with the check up and I survived that ordeal too.

(Seventh recording session begins:)

David: Did you have any dreams during the war? Do you dream of the war today? Or after the war?

Charlie: Yes. In the war, we were dreaming always about good, nice things. Dreaming about the good things which we have in Poland. Only after the war, many, many years I used to wake up at night and screaming. Always the same type of dreams. That Germans are after me, they chasing me and they almost capturing me. Now, I am always escaping and hiding. And, I used to scream. My wife always used to shake my arm, she woke me up. I said "What, what, what is it?" And that dream were going on at least for 20 years. Every once in a while, if I have some pressure, at night I used to dream, scream loud and cry until lately the situation improved. Even in the last years I was dreaming every once in a while and I'm screaming still. Not so badly anymore.

CHAPTER 14

CHARLIE ARRIVES IN AMERICA

Relocation was a primary issue for many survivors of the Holocaust. Of the countries open to Jewish refugees, there were policies and quotas involved. Survivors were left to languish in displaced persons camps facing both the uncertainty of where they would go next as well as when the relocation would occur. Survivors would begin the application process to multiple destinations and settle in the first place they were accepted.

An applicant needed to list a sponsor in the host country. Survivors had to search for family members or organizations who would provide for their passage and support or employ them in their new countries. Many countries were wary of accepting refugees, anticipating the refugees were at risk for becoming destitute and burden the public with their needs.

Finally, all refugees had to show they were in good health and fit to work before they would be accepted. These restrictions were devastating to survivors. Many survivors had lost their families and did not have sponsors. They were weak and injured during the war and were not in good enough health to work. These restrictions frustrated and stagnated the survivors' effort to restart their lives and provided evidence that the world did not care about them and did not comprehend their reality.

In the Lampertheim displaced persons camp, Charlie worked on reuniting with his family and began planning his resettlement. On August 23, 1946, Charlie wrote in a letter to the Sierpcer Relief Committee:

> One can no longer remain there *(in Sierpc);* I have left everything and came over here. I live here in a UNRRA camp. I have also hopes to come to America, but it has now become more difficult. It is possible that you can have some influence in the consulate of the relief committee; with this, you can help me. My papers are already with the consulate, but I still have no visa. My papers were sent to me by my cousin, his address: A. Wolman,[113] 24-53 64th St., Brooklyn, NY. I really would like to come to America; there is no future for life here.

Charlie waited more than three years before relocating to America. On December 14, 1948, he was issued a health clearance card to emigrate.[114] During that time, as there had been no progress in obtaining a visa to the United States, he applied for entry to other countries. On February 4, 1949, an immigration card was issued for him by the American Joint Distribution Committee to emigrate to Australia.[115] Charlie had also considered emigrating to Israel.

While Charlie had family in America willing to sponsor him as early as in 1946, it took three years for his visa to get approved. Finally, on

---

[113] Pesa Kadecki's sister, Rachel married Moshe Hersz Wolman, their oldest son was Abram Wolman. Abe Wolman is Mark Hallerman's, grandfather.

[114] Health Clearance: December 14, 1948, issued in Lampertheim displaced persons camp. Record courtesy of Joel Lelonek.

[115] American Joint Distribution Committee, Emigration card for Szaja Lelonek, February 4, 1949. International Tracing Service courtesy of USHMM.

April 13, 1949, Passover eve, Shayah Lelonek, 34 years old, was registered on a role of displaced persons to depart from a resettlement center in Butzbach, Germany for emigration, VISA #6632/52.[116] Eleven days later, on April 24, 1949, he set sail on the ship USAT General Black departing from Bremerhaven, Germany to the port of New York, NY. He was sponsored by a wealthy first cousin, Morris Kadetz, who successfully ran a dress factory. Although the ship manifest recorded that he intended to stay at his cousin's house on 15 Coram Street, Taunton, Massachusetts, he instead stayed with his maternal uncle William Kadetsky in Manhattan.[117]

Charlie's eleven-day voyage across the Atlantic ocean ended on May 4, 1949,[118] arriving in New York, NY. The ship docked at Ellis Island, where the majority of new immigrants got off. Since Charlie had a sponsor, he stayed on the ship and he got off in Manhattan, at a small immigration center in midtown, at about 43 St. He received a brief physical exam, a simpler exam than the ones administered at Ellis Island and was greeted there by his maternal uncle, William Kadetsky. He moved in with William while he adjusted to life in New York City and started working as a tailor.

USAT USS General W. M. Black

---

[116] Nominal role of persons departing from a resettlement Center in Butzbach on April 13, 1949, for emigration. International Tracing Service courtesy of USHMM.
[117] Morris Kadetz was Charlie Lelonek's first cousin. Pesa Lelonek's older brother, Abraham Kadetsky's son.
[118] ITS inquiry card (31408151-0-1). Courtesy of USHMM.

A year later, Ben and Esther Schweitzer, hosted a party in Manhattan for families who used to live in the same region of Poland. Charlie attended and there he met Sylvia Haskel, daughter of William Haskel and Hinda Appelbaum. The Haskel family had immigrated from Poland to America in 1906 and established themselves as the leaders in the monument and granite industry. The family's businesses, "S. Haskel and Sons," an industrial granite supplier, as well as their retail monument outlet "Shastone," were the United States' largest suppliers of granite to the monument industry on the east coast. Shastone granites were used for building exterior work, memorials, mausoleums, and monuments. The family had quarries in New England, Norway, Sweden, Finland, and Germany. S. Haskel and Sons was the granite supplier for many buildings nationwide including the Empire State Building, the Chrysler Building, the Museum of Natural History in New York and the President Warren G. Harding Memorial. Sylvia's parents were supporters of the Jewish community. The Haskel family originated from Bendin, Poland, and the Appelbaum family from Sierpc, Poland. They supported the charities for their hometowns starting in the early 1900's and continued after the Holocaust. They supported Jewish education in Europe and Israel. In 1924, they hosted a fundraiser led by Rav Avraham Yitzchak Kook, the Chief Ashkenazi Rabbi in Israel, Rabbi Moses Mordechai Epstein, the dean of the Slobodka Yeshiva and Rabbi Abraham Bear Shapiro, the chief rabbi of Kovno. After the Holocaust, the family sponsored survivors and Yizkor gatherings.[119]

Charlie and Sylvia had much in common. Sylvia's mother's family originated from Sierpc, where Charlie had grown up. The families had known each other before the Appelbaum family immigrated to America in 1902. In America, Charlie worked with Ben Schweitzer, the

---

[119] Communities came together on a day significant to their European town to memorialize the victims and deceased survivors.

husband of Sylvia's maternal aunt Esther Schweitzer nee Appelbaum, making custom dresses for affluent clientele.

During the party, Charlie asked Sylvia to go for a walk with him. They walked and talked for hours. Sylvia recalls that it was very cold out and there were icicles hanging. Charlie was "very charming, telling stories of his experiences." They married on March 4, 1951, at the Paradise wedding hall. Since Charlie's parents and siblings was unable to attend the wedding, they held a party in Israel the same night. Charlie's uncle and aunt, William and Dora Kadetsky, stood under the chuppah[120] with Charlie.[121]

All of Charlie's documents prior to his arrival in America record his name as Szaja. To his countryman and siblings, he was known as Shayah. Before his wedding, he Americanized his name to Charles Lelonek. He became a naturalized citizen on November 11, 1954.

Charlie had an amazing work ethic and desire to support his family. He opened his own clothing store, "C & S Clothing," which was named for Charlie and Sylvia, in the Bay Ridge area of Brooklyn. He worked 6 days a week. Every day, he left early in the morning and came home from work late at night. When his sons were old enough, they worked in the store along aside him. He retired in 1988.

Charlie and Sylvia had seven children; Joel, Cliff, Robin, Michael, Steven, David and Richard. Their 2 oldest children were named in honor of relatives connected to Charlie's journey. In memory of Esther Schweitzer's first husband, Jack Richgat and in recognition of the role Esther played in facilitating the meeting of Charlie and Sylvia, Joel was given Jack's Hebrew name Yaakov Yonah. Cliff's Hebrew name is Chaim, in memory of Charlie's brother, Chaim, who disappeared after being arrested by the Russians in 1940.

---

[120] Jewish wedding canopy.
[121] Beth McGreen, identifying her grandfather in a photo provided by Rachel Lelonek that was copied from Miriam Lelonek.

CHAPTER 15

CHARLIE'S LAST DAY
BY JOEL, DAVID AND RICHARD LELONEK

On Rosh HaShanah 5754, 1994, Charlie wanted to go to the synagogue. After all, he had always welcomed the new year and it was important for him to attend services. Being part of an Orthodox synagogue, the Flatbush Park Jewish Center, he would walk to shul during the holidays. Unfortunately, it had been a difficult year for Charlie, as he was losing his battle with cancer. He was weak and unable to walk the distance of just under a mile from his house. His son, Richard, knew how important this was to Charlie and drove him to synagogue. Richard felt it made more sense to drive Charlie to synagogue than for him not to go at all.

In addition to the main sanctuary, The Flatbush Park Jewish Center had also set their gymnasium up to accommodate the High Holiday prayer services. Rabbi David Halpern and others rotated locations throughout the services.

The synagogue was very busy and there were no tallisim available near the main sanctuary to be draped over Charlie's shoulders. With his dad in a wheelchair, Richard pushed Charlie into the sanctuary. Charlie then asked Richard to get him a tallis and Richard went to the gymnasium to find one. Richard quickly found an available tallis and hurried back to the main sanctuary where he draped it over his father's shoulders. It was time for the shofar to be blown. Charlie heard the sound, looked at Richard and said, "Okay, let's go home." Clearly, hearing the blasts of the shofar was of paramount importance to Charlie. He had wanted to welcome in the new year.

Charlie's health quickly deteriorated between Rosh HaShanah and Yom Kippur. His family lovingly cared for him around the clock. As Charlie's pain medication was increased, his ability to perform simple functions and maintain consciousness decreased dramatically. By the eve of Yom Kippur, the family felt Charlie needed even more care and were about to look into hospice programs.

After attending Yom Kippur services with his family in Long Island, David drove to Brooklyn to join his brother Steven with their dad. When David arrived at his parent's house, their mom was in synagogue praying the Mussaf service.[122] He entered his parent's room, where Charlie was lying down, quietly moaning in bed. David was concerned, unsure if Charlie was conscious. Steven reported that Charlie had moaned most of the day. David gently called out, "Dad are you okay?" and his dad immediately perked up. Seeing David, he smiled and asked, "David, you are here?" David reassured him he was and asked again if he was okay. Charlie responded he was fine and inquired about why David was concerned. David told him that he had heard him moaning and was worried that he might be in pain. Charlie assured David he was not, but as soon as he stopped speaking he began to softly moan again. He kept his eyes closed most of the time; opening them rarely and then only slightly.

Charlie then asked David, "Where is Sylvia?" David explained his mom was at the synagogue. "Why do you ask?" Charlie replied, "The angels have come to get me, but I told them I can't go yet. I have to say goodbye to Sylvia. I told them they would have to wait." Steven and David were standing together with their father. David told him,

---

[122] An added prayer service for the Sabbath, new month and holidays.

"Mom will be home soon" and asked him to try to wait for her. While waiting for Sylvia, David sat by his father's side.

About a half hour later Sylvia returned home from synagogue. David heard her taking out her keys and met her at the door. He relayed what Charlie had said to prepare her for the tough moments ahead. She began to sob and went to his bedside.

Sylvia called out, "Charlie, here I am." Charlie opened his eyes wide and replied, "The angels came to get me but I told them they had to wait for you. I have to say goodbye to Sylvia." He then closed his eyes again. Steven, David, and Sylvia were crying. Sylvia bent down and gently stroked Charlie's hand telling him, "I'm here Charlie. You've said goodbye to me. It's okay to go." She then laid down beside him and he soon fell asleep.

Early the next morning, September 16, 1994, at 8am, Steven called David crying, saying "I think Dad is dead. Come over quickly!" David jumped in his car and drove to Brooklyn. He checked Charlie's vitals and confirmed his passing.

What a remarkable scene: to spend the last moments of life at home surrounded by family, to ask permission from your spouse before going to olam haba,[123] and to be accompanied by angels to the next world. Charlie had atoned and asked for G-d's forgiveness. As Yom Kippur was coming to a close, his soul attained the spiritual purity and atonement of the day. His soul ascended to olam haba as pure as it had entered the world.

Rosh HaShanah and Yom Kippur were very special to Charlie. Charlie described the first Yom Kippur in 1939 after the Nazis invaded Poland. Then, five years later, on the eve of Rosh HaShanah September 16, 1944, Charlie crossed the Vistula to join his comrades fighting in the Warsaw Uprising against the Nazis and continued

---

[123] The world to come.

fighting on Yom Kippur. He was captured by the Nazis and reported missing in action and presumed dead. His family sat shivah for him. But G-d had different plans for Charlie. Charlie was granted exactly 50 additional years to fulfill his mission in life, dying on September 16, 1994, after Yom Kippur.

Lelonek family in Lampertheim: sitting right to left; Yitzchak Mayer, Pesa, Miriam. Standing; Moshe holding his daughter Ester, Rachel Lelonek nee Segal, Yosef Lazinsky, Bluma Lazinsky nee Lelonek, Charlie Shayah Lelonek, Tzvi Lelonek.

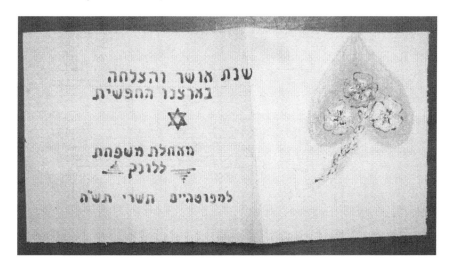

Jewish New Year card drawn by Rachel Lelonek nee Segal, for Rosh HaShanah 1948 (5708), 5 months after the establishment of the state of Israel. The card was sent with a letter from Moshe Lelonek in the Lampertheim displaced persons camp to the Sierpc Relief Committee in NY. The card reads: "A year with wealth and success in our free land. Wishes from the Lelonek family to your families. Tishrei 5708."

Sierpc survivors Yizkor gathering to commemorate the 5,000 victims who were murdered from Sierpc. The hanging sign reads: "For the Sierpc Holies exiled in Germany." The monument reads; "Remember the 5,000 holy souls from Sierpc who died a hateful death by the hands of the murdering Germans from the years 1940-1943. May their memory be eternal. God should avenge their blood. 19 of Adar 5709, March 20, 1949." Charlie is standing in the bottom row, second from left.

PART III

BLUMA LAZINSKY'S TESTIMONY

INTRODUCTION

Bluma Lazinsky was Charlie's older sister. Bluma Lazinsky wrote her reparation request from Germany, on January 24, 1964. In 2000, I visited with her and we discussed our family history. She shared her reparations request when I inquired about what happened to family during the Holocaust. The following is a translation of her reparation request. I have included it to give a different perspective of the Lelonek family's experiences. Bluma's account gives insight into the struggle of survivors to claim reparations for their injuries, lost wages and property.

CHAPTER 16

BLUMA'S REPARATION REQUEST
BY BLUMA LAZINSKY

To the point:

At the outbreak of the German Polish War,[124] I lived with my husband, who was a tailor, in Sierpc.

After the occupation of Sierpc by the German troops we were expelled from our house and I came with my husband to Warsaw, passing Nowy Dwór. At the end of December 1939, I fled with my husband due to the anti-Semitic German laws in the German occupied Poland. We fled to the Russian occupied front. We arrived in Bialystok, where we were arrested by the Russians for illegally crossing the line of demarcation and dragged to Siberia.

At the crossing of the line demarcation I was mistreated heavily by uniformed Germans and was hit with a heavy metal stick on the fingers of my left hand, was badly wounded. I bandaged *(my wound)*.

In Siberia, there was no medical help, and my wound was not treated medically. Since that time, my left hand is crippled. Then we were brought to the Arkhangelsk Oblast where my husband was forced

---

[124] The invasion of Poland on September 1, 1939, starting World War II.

to do heavy work in the labor camp, Poyaminka. We constantly were suffering from hunger, heavy cold and humidity.

The lodging and the clothing situation were terrible. The moral and bodily burdening were very heavy.

At the beginning of 1942 we were brought to the area of Konjevo[125] and in 1946 from there repatriated to Poland. We came to Stettin and from there in the DP camp Lampertheim, where we also were on the right day, on January 1, 1947.[126] In 1949, I immigrated to Israel from Lampertheim with my husband.

Already in Lampertheim, I inquired whether I would have right for indemnification against Germany. I received the information from the administration of the camp that prosecuted persons who have been in Russia did not have any right to claim reparations against Germany.

Also, after my immigration to Israel, where it was generally known that the Russian prosecuted persons did not have any rights to claim reparations against Germany and that the indemnification officials and courts rejected such demands, I received the information that I did not have any right against Germany.

Still before the end of the legal delay of demand, I was directed to the URO *(United Restitution Organization[127])* in Haifa where submitted my prosecution fate and received the information, that it was useless

---

[125] There is one village with the name Konevo in the Arkhangelsk Oblast. Konevo, Plesetskiy, Arkhangelsk Oblast, Russia.

[126] "Stichtag" (Jan 1, 1947) is the qualifying date for the indemnification. The applicant had to be present in Germany at that time to be considered for indemnification. This date has later been changed to Dec 31, 1952. See for example: http://www.wollheim-memorial.de/de/bundesentschaedigungsgesetz_1956

[127] The United Restitution Organization (URO) was established in 1948 as a legal aid service to help victims of Nazi persecution living outside Germany in making restitution and indemnification claims against Germany and Austria. The URO has served over 250,000 clients. It helped Jews, Roma, and other victims of Nazi crimes. At its most expansive, the URO maintained twenty-nine offices in fifteen countries around the world. -Wikipedia

to claim and that the URO could not take over the representation.

I am a person without legal knowledge, and relied on the information I received from the URO and for that reason I did not bring forward my claim during the legal period.

On January 9, 1964 I have made a declaration under oath at the URO in Haifa for my sister in law Rachel Lelonek in her indemnification case Munich 86914. On this occasion I learned that the highest court in Germany did decide in favor of the prosecuted persons from Russia and I asked the official of the URO, for him to inquire on my behalf. I received an appointment on January 15, 1964.

From the above mentioned, it can be deduced that I am not at fault for not meeting the legal duty of claiming. Therefore, I ask to be reconsidered in the previous situation and I also claim indemnification for damage to my health.

Personal signature: Bluma Lazinsky

Signed: Haifa January 24, 1964 Dr. Richard Jelinak

PART IV

MOSHE LELONEK'S TESTIMONY

INTRODUCTION

The following was written by Moshe Lelonek, Charlie's younger brother, for his great grandchildren's "roots work." Moshe's grandson, Oren Yagoda provided it to me. The roots work is a school assignment for children to research and interview their parents and grandparents about their family history.

Moshe's account offers another perspective on the Lelonek family's reality during the war. He describes the family's journey and settlement in Israel. His account addresses the gap in Charlie's interview about what happened to the Lelonek family when they were deported from Bialystok to Siberia.

CHAPTER 17

MOSHE'S TESTIMONY
BY MOSHE LELONEK

I was born in Poland in the town Sierpc near Warsaw, on February 1, 1922, the fifth child among seven siblings. My father was a Zionist. With a number of Jews, he established a group and collected money to build a Yehuda Hebrew school. They brought teachers from Lithuania, who could teach Hebrew in school. I was in the first graduating class of the school. In 1939, war broke out between Germany and Poland, and in three days the Germans conquered Poland. After the occupation of Poland, they drove us out of our town; we boarded the train to Warsaw and stayed there until they began to concentrate Jews in ghettos. My brother *(Charlie)* and I took backpacks and fled to Bialystok, where we were for a number of months. After several months, in the early morning, the secret police came to our house and told us to come out, they are taking us somewhere. Outside was a van that took us to the train station in the city. They put us on train carriages, which were cattle cars. After a four-week train ride to northern Russia cities in Arkhangelsk *(Siberia),* we were housed in barracks in the woods. We worked cutting wood in the forest and in return every day we received bread and soup. The temperature was 45 degrees below 0. We stayed in this camp until 1943. Rachel was also in this camp and I met her there. In 1943, we were moved to the center of the city of Gorky, Russia but there were German bombs. They decided not leave us there and brought us to Vaad *(Vaksa)*. I worked there as a supplier of a factory that supplied clothes and shoes to the Red Army. In Vaad, I married Rachel by civil registration office of the Russian government. On March 22, 1944, my daughter Ester was born. After the war was confirmed over, we returned to Poland, and we concentrated in the town of Nowa Ruda[128] [129] in a "kibbutz" where the agency gathered all the Jews who wanted to immigrate to Israel. The agency organized false papers like we were German citizens. In 1946, we came to Germany and stayed there until 1948. We stayed in the group of Jews who were Holocaust survivors. In this town *(Lampertheim)*, I was among those who set up a Hebrew school and I ran it. The students were ages 5 to 15, they were studying for the first time in their lives, because before then, they were in concentration camps. In addition, I volunteered for a committee that welcomed people who wanted to fight and serve in the IDF for Israel's War of Independence. At the end of 1948, we went to Marseille. We were there for a number of months waiting for winter to pass, so we can go on a ship to go up to the Land *(of Israel)*. In early 1949, we boarded the ship, "Marathon" and within a week we got to the state of Israel. They put us up in an immigrant camp in Pardes Hannah, which was previously a British army camp. Tova, my sister, was a pioneer and emigrated to Israel in 1935, lived in a house in Newe Haifa and she

---

[128] http://en.wikipedia.org/wiki/Nowa_Ruda

[129] The following family members list Nowa Ruda as a wartime location: David Lazinsky (b. 1896, tailor, son of Szaja, Gitla) and Bluma Lazenska (b. 1912, daughter of Majer (Icek), Pesa), Icek (b. 1884, son of Abram, Matla) and Pesa Lelonek (b. 1890, daughter of Szaja), Grzegorz Lelonek (b. 1929 most likely Hersz/Tzvi son of Icek, Pesa), Estera Lelonek (b. 1944), Maria Lelonek (b. 1921), Michal Lelonek (b. 1926, tailor, son of Icek, Pesa), Raisa Lelonek (b. 1926 daughter of Wiktor, Szyfra). Source: Polish Survivors. A database of Polish Holocaust survivors who went back to Poland after the war and registered themselves in local Jewish committees. This data refers to Jews who were living in the Warsaw province before the war and/or after the war, and does not contain survivors who were in Warsaw itself. Central Committee of the Jews in Poland, Department of Statistics and Registration or Department of Landsmanshaft in the JHI Archives. Record courtesy of the USHMM.

took us into her home. In one room there lived two families. I was looking for a house in Haifa and found a house that the Arabs had abandoned in the war. We moved to a rented apartment in Romema, which was government housing for immigrants. In 1956, we bought a house on Azar 8 in Newe, part of a government mass housing project. On April 1, 1956, Chaim was born. In 1949, I started working with the electric company, connecting electricity to homes, where I worked until I retired in 1989. I bought a house in July 1967, 26 Pinsker Street. Rachel received compensation funds from the Germans and the sale of a previous home. And since then we live in this house.

PART V

LETTERS FROM THE LAMPERTHEIM DISPLACED PERSONS CAMP

INTRODUCTION

I visited the YIVO archives in Manhattan, to view the rare Yizkor book *Zaml Book Fun Sierpcer Shairit HaChurban* co-edited by Szaja Lelonek. There, I discovered another holding for Sierpc and requested to see it. They brought two boxes filled with over a thousand letters written by Sierpc survivors to the Sierpcer Relief Committee in New York. Overwhelmed with emotion, I held my family's original letters in their envelopes. In the collection were 33 letters written by the Lelonek family from 1946-1949, in Yiddish, German and Polish. They describe life in the Lampertheim displaced persons camp, the establishment of the state of Israel, the emotional toll the uncertainty of where they will live and when they will be able to continue their lives. With the help of JewishGen volunteers, many of the letters have been translated. To introduce the letters, I have reprinted the chapter from *Memorial Book of Sierpc, Poland* about the relief committee titled "Mister United Sierpc Relief."

CHAPTER 18

MISTER UNITED SIERPC RELIEF[130] [131]

BY YEHUDA LEIB MINTZ

When one discusses or writes about Sierpcer Jews, their life and economic creativity, their societal and cultural activities, the four Sierpc Landsmanshaft[132] organizations in New York play a very important role. These are the old Sierpcer Gemilut Chasadim,[133] the Independent Sierpc Young Men, its ladies' division called the Sierpcer Ladies Auxiliary, and the Sierpc Branch 42 of the Jewish National Workers Union.

Each of those organizations had its own role in various realms of Jewish societal life in America, as well as in Europe, the Land of Israel, and, of late, the State of Israel.

The most noble of their activities, as well as the most prominent, was the founding of the United Sierpc Relief - the Sierpc help

[130] Reprinted with permission from the coordinator of the JewishGen Yizkor Book Project, Lance Ackerfeld and Dorothy Lipsky.

[131] Talmi, E., (1959) *Kehilat Sierpc; Sefer Zikaron*, Tel Aviv, Israel.
Talmi, E., Krisch, S., Lipsky, D. K., Landau, J., & Weingarten, A. (2014). *Memorial Book of Sierpc, Poland: Translation of Kehilat Sierpc; Sefer Zikaron*. New York: JewishGen. pages 543-545.

[132] A fraternal organization made up of Jewish immigrants from the same region.

[133] Lit. Loving kindness. A community charity organization.

organization that was created by all four organizations with the goal of assisting Sierpc natives wherever they are found, whether in Sierpc itself (before the great misfortune of Hitler, may his name be blotted out), in the countries where the bitter fate had brought them, or in their new home in the Land of Israel.

It is natural that in a book about Sierpc, mention must be made of that united organization - the United Sierpc Relief Organization. Its founders included Mordechai Tzvi Mintz of blessed memory - the Sierpc teacher who educated a generation of Zionists and Hebraists in the town and continued his teaching work in America; Shlomo Loeb (Lobashka) of blessed memory, who belonged to the Zionist Workers' camp both in Sierpc and in New York, and, together with his late wife Pesha, spent all of his years involved in charitable activities; and Yaakov Sand of blessed memory a long-time member and leader of the Sierpc Young Men's Organization.

It is obvious that in order to function properly, an organization must have workers - people who are willing to dedicate their time and energy to the goals of raising the necessary financial means, maintaining contact with the needy people and distributing the assistance to those in need. To move forward, the activists required the driving force that would propel the organization forward. That driving force was no longer a physical driving force alone - let us say an electric motor that would be set in motion once and continue to go. The driving force that was needed for this type of relief work must be spiritual - a driving force that springs forth from the depths of the soul of the individual personalities who possessed warm hearts and fine senses of sensitivity to the ideal goal for which the help organization was created.

The United Sierpc Relief Committee had the fortune of having that very internal drive embodied in the personality of Mr. Max Sina[134] - a

---

[134] Many letters written by Lelonek family members from the Lampertheim displaced persons camp address Max Sina.

long time member and activist in the Sierpc Young Men's Organization. A book about Sierpc and its Jews would simply be imperfect if it failed to mention Max Sina and his good deeds amongst us. Standing near to him in our joint work - I as the financial secretary and my wife Rashe and Mordechai Reshotko[135] as corresponding secretaries of the Sierpc Relief, of which Max Sina was the president – we often admired his singular deep dedication to the work for the Sierpcers. For him, the word "Sierpcer" was a magic word that instilled a life spirit - a soul - in him, an inspiration that reflected off of him and influenced those with whom he worked together.

When a Sierpcer requested assistance, or if he merely heard that there was someone who required assistance, Mr. Sina would immediately feel a great sense of responsibility and would strive to help without any additional clarification of qualifications - the word "Sierpcer" was already a sufficient qualification. This was just like the word "Jew" to Rabbi Levi Yitzchak Berditchever of blessed memory, for whom he would always serve a righteous intercessor before the Master of the Universe. Can one ask a mother about the qualifications, or positive and negative traits of her child? It is her child - she loves him - and that is all. That was the very relationship that Max Sina had with his dispersed Sierpc fellow natives, wherever they might be found. With him, there was no cause for doubts. If he took something on, if he set off on a designated path to help his fellow natives, there would never be a case of "return us back" - always forward, forward, and never back.

It seems that Max Sina himself had for a long time not been vigorous and healthy. However, he displayed exceptional strength when it came to his beloved relief work for Sierpcers. I can never forget the warm evenings and nights that we spent in the basement of my

---

[135] Mordechai Max Reshotko was the brother in law of Charlie's first cousin, Sara Malka Lelonek. Many letters written by Lelonek family members from the Lampertheim displaced persons camp address Max Reshotko and make references to shared family.

house in Brooklyn sorting the clothing and food to make packages to send to the Sierpcer refugees in Germany, Italy, France, the Land of Israel, and Africa. He himself was a capable man who could have permitted himself some personal comforts after a hard workday in New York. Instead of traveling for a weekend to his summer home by the sea to cool off and rest, he came to our house where everything was collected and undertook the work that was holy to him. If it was too late to go home, he would spend the night with us and wake up very early in the morning to catch the train to go home. He never complained about others who were not as willing as he was to work. He carried out his holy duty that certainly brought him spiritual enjoyment.

When it was decided to undertake the activity for the Sierpcer Relief, for various reasons of which here is not the place to write, Max Sina was conducting a "Sierpcer Relief" on a small scale by himself. He obtained money, of course putting in no small amount of his own cash, and sent it to where he thought there was the need.

When the first refugees from Germany began to arrive in America, he himself conducted the individual assistance activity for them. He found work for those he could, and if it there was the need, he would take them into his own shop. They learned the trade of sewing on the machine, and then they were employed by him or by someone else. On many occasions, he spent entire evenings with the students in the shop, in order to avoid a meeting with his partner or with the Workers Union. When it was possible, one of the new arrivals would find a paternal accommodation at Mr. Sina's house during his first days in New York, and receive warm maternal treatment from his prominent wife.

When at last, the undertaking of creating a Yizkor book to perpetuate the memories of the martyrs of Sierpc came to the fore through the initiative of our fellow natives in Israel, and a leading hand was needed in order to turn to the fellow natives in America for financial assistance as well as to collect written material and documents or data from historical works, Max Sina took upon himself the mission to conduct this work and to do everything that was needed, to make it possible for our fellow natives in Tel Aviv to do their work. Due to his poor state of health, he had already retired from his private business. On account of his weakness on his feet and his poor vision, and after several serious operations including on the eyes, he suffered from several serious accidents that caused him no small amount of additional physical suffering. However, none of this held him back from continuing with the work. He continued to connect with everyone by telephone, to call meetings at his home, and to do everything that he could do to help actualize the Sierpc Yizkor book, which had lately become his purpose in life.

That intensive dedication to his work to help the Sierpcers had its influence upon those surrounding him, so that it was almost impossible to refuse his requests to become involved and do work, even in cases where one was not in complete agreement with him. There was something about the dedication of Max Sina that stood higher than any cold reckoning and accounting.

That characteristic of Max Sina shone like a ray of light through all the years of our mutual work for the Sierpcer Relief until his final undertaking to create the Sierpc Yizkor book - and from that stems our respect for Mr. Max Sina, "Mr. United Sierpc Relief."

Unfortunately, he did not merit in seeing the Sierpc Yizkor book. He passed away on May 20, 1959, corresponding to the 12th of Iyar, 5719. May his memory be a blessing!

CHAPTER 19

LELONEK FAMILY'S LETTERS
YITZCHAK MAYER'S LETTERS

Yitzchak Mayer Lelonek, 64 years old in 1947, written in Yiddish

March 26, 1947

Dear friends and countrymen!

Two days ago we received two packages from the Sierpc Relief Committee. We thank you very much for your initiative in helping out your fellow citizens in this difficult period of our lives. We will make good use of the things. We may be able to reciprocate at some point. Now, my dear friends, I can write you that we are all healthy, and waiting impatiently for the time when we will leave this place. I can share with you that I have married off my daughter Manya to Yitzchak Hutnik. He is a young man from Sierpc, you probably know him. It is very hard these days to marry off your children, but we have already overcome the worst. I am here now with my wife and 17-year-old son. He is studying a bit in a vocational school. During the war, he couldn't study.

My son, Shayah, considers going to America, soon. Could be, that you will meet him. And, what I will do? I don't know it, yet. I have to wait and to endure the fate of the entire Jewish people! I'm already 64 years old and unable to work. And my wife shall stay healthy. My son Moshe married in Russia land, he has a 2½-year-old little girl, already. He works in the school. From my daughter, Bluma, I got a thin letter. Everybody is there in Lampertheim, waiting to leave. I have a big favor to ask of you, to send me, kindly, a letter! I am, finally, a Jew from Sierpc, who knows all of you since childhood, and what's been left to me after the great catastrophe of the Jewish people. Don't forget that I, in my older years, feel very connected just with you! I greet the Sierpcer Committee and all countrymen very warmly, send them also regards from my family, we wish you all good things, also a good and kosher Passover.

Your friend and countryman,

Yitzchak Mayer Lelonek from Sierpc

September 4, 1947, Lampertheim

Honored Relief Committee,

I can inform you that today I received the parcel and I thank you all for not forgetting your hometown people that are now in Germany. The new year *(Rosh HaShanah)* will be starting soon and we wish you life and good health, and may we and you soon be redeemed from the exile. We have no other news. We are all in good health and hope to hear good news from you too. We send regards to the whole Committee and I thank you many times for not forgetting us.

From me,

Yitzchak Mayer Lelonek from Sierpc

Undated Letter. Lampertheim:

Best Friend Max Sina,

I'm letting you know, that I received your dear letter with 5 dollars correctly and I thank the whole committee for not forgetting us. Now comes the new year *(Rosh HaShanah)* and we wish you health and life in the new year, regards to the whole community from your friend Yitzchak Mayer and family.

Yitzchak Mayer Lelonek, who wishes you everything good.

A special regards to Max Sina and from the whole family who wish you a good year.

From your friend,

Yitzchak Mayer Lelonek

April 13, 1948,

Dear friend Max Sina,

Today, I received the parcel, which you sent me, correctly, and I thank you very much. Why are you writing me so little? I'd like to know everything that's happening. On my place, everything is as always, meanwhile, we didn't get on, we would have known, to find a place, but, unfortunately, everything is difficult to come in, everything. We have to wait until we will be helped to get a home. There's no other important news. We are greeting you with your wife and the whole family special regards to your sister, Chavele, and to the whole family Rozen and to the whole Sierpcer committee and we wish all of you a happy holiday and we wish all of you everything good.

From your friend,

Yitzchak Mayer Lelonek

May 28, 1948

Good friend Max Sina,

We let you know that we received your parcel and I thank all of you for your good treatment. God shall help, for you don't forget us. And you and also we shall be helped, that we no longer need, but do have a home already! There is no more important news. We are greeting you, Max Sina and the whole committee and we wish you everything good,

From your friend,

Yitzchak Mayer Lelonek

BLUMA'S LETTERS

Bluma Lazinsky, 34 years old in 1946, written in Yiddish.

Lampertheim, September 30/9, 1946

Dear friend Mordche,

First, I let you know you that this letter is written to you by the friend of your sister, Ruchelain, Bluma Lelonek from Sierpc. We are staying in the American Zone in Germany. The name of the town is Lampertheim, we have arrived here around the new year *(Rosh HaShanah)*. We have previously been in Poland and during the war, in Russia. I wanted to write you from Poland, but I did not have an address. Today, I got your address, and I write you right away.

Dear Friend,

Certainly you know about our survival from 1939 until this day, we were traveling on foot with our walking staffs, homeless. Our suffering might not have ended yet; we still do not have a place. We have not yet obtained and we do not know how long this will last. Until now we live under dire circumstances and we do not obtain any aid from the

Americans. Therefore, I am compelled to turn to you to help us for food and clothing. We could not bring anything with us, our journey has been very difficult. It is not agreeable for me to write this, but at the moment we cannot help ourselves; we have already asked sister Tova and cousin Baruch in Palestine, they wanted to help us, but it was impossible. Please, do not send any money...

I conclude my letter, for now, stay healthy, accept my regards and give my regards to your wife and your children, greet all Sierpcers, and regards from my parents, my sister and my brothers. My husband greets you and all Sierpcers, even if he does not know them.

From me,

Bluma Lelonek and from my husband, David Lazinsky.

Lampertheim, December 17, 1946

Dear friend Mordche,

Today I received a little a little piece of paper from you, in which you write, that you haven't understood my first letter. Yes, it is true, I, actually, do believe, that you are not able to understand such letters, because people, who live in good conditions, cannot realize and don't want to understand, how life in the camp is, without a home, without means to live and so on... You all, who present the Sierpcer Relief Committee, what do you understand? To respond to long, painful letters with small, cold two words! And therefore, the question read: What have all of you achieved, already? Whom did you give a help, already? There isn't more than dry and cold relationship to be seen from you! That it is, on paper you're declaiming as a Sierpcer Relief Committee - well, that's true - paper is patient! You can write, what you want. And it is: The rich one does not believe the hungry one and I won't write more about this because my heart feels too much hurt. Well, anyway, I believe, that you, possibly, will understand this letter, and with a good will, you actually, will understand… I close my letter with greetings to the Sierpcer Relief Committee and to you and family.

From me,

Bluma Lelonek-Lazinsky.

July 22, 1947

Summary:

To Sierpcer friends,

We received the food parcel. Thank you very much.

I am happy to have lived to see the day we have our own country. It is only very, very sad that our 6 million martyrs didn't live to have the joy to see that day. Because of that, my joy is clouded; many of my nearest and dearest dreamed and fought for this moment and didn't live to see it, although they longed so much for this land and so much blood has been spilled for it. Now I hope to be able to reconstruct my life there and build a future.

Regards to dear friends Max and Dinah, and dear friend Mordecai Reshotko and wishes they all meet in the future in the land of Israel.

David and Bluma Lazinsky

November 25, 1947

Summary:

Dear friend Mordecai and family,

Thank you for taking an interest in our situation. We understand that you don't have much time to write and read letters because you are very busy.

We received a letter from Hersch Mechel[136] from Argentina saying that Chaim married on November 1. Otherwise, we have no special news.

We had hoped in the course of last year that they would be able to come to America.

Now we hope that the UN general assembly will decide about the Jewish land and they will be able to finally go back to our own country.

We are fed up with waiting and having to stretch out their hand begging for charity. We want to live with dignity like everyone else, abandon this gypsy life of wandering and finally settle, build, and create.

Bluma and David Lazinsky

May 12, 1948

Dear Sierpcer friends!

This week we received the parcel with food, which you sent to us on March 16. It arrived in perfect order, we thank you very much. And we are doing our best to inform you immediately because you shall not be in doubt, whether it has arrived. At the same time, I can write you, that Baruch Lelonek from Palestine is staying in our place. He is staying with his American friends. He already visited us several times, also the first days of Passover and even today he is staying with us in the camp, as well. He came here as an embassy of his direction. He already has

---

[136] The letter addresses Mordechai Max Reshotko. Max had a brother, Hersch Michael Reshotko who was married Sara Malka Lelonek, a first cousin of Charlie's. Hersch and Sara Reshotko emigrated to Argentina before World War II with their son Chaim. Presumably, the letter is referencing Hersch's son, Chaim, getting married.

been more than four months here, and he prepares to go home, soon. A special regard to Mordechai Reshotko. Baruch gladly would have written something, but he is very busy. He also greets all Sherptser, who remember him. No more news by us. You, certainly, read the newspapers, so you can see, that meanwhile everything is in change. We live and hope, and we don't know what our end will be. No more important things, we are greeting you very cordially, a special regard to Mr. Max Sina and Mordechai Reshotko, also to all Sierpcer countrymen. Please answer!

From us,

David and Bluma Lazinsky.

CHARLIE'S LETTERS

Charlie Lelonek, 32 years old in 1946, written in Yiddish.

August 23, 1946:

Dear Mordechai,

You will probably wonder at receiving a letter from me. The one writing to you is Shayah Lelonek, Yitzchak Mayer Lelonek's son. Hersch Mechel, your brother, married Sarah Malka Lelonek, the daughter of uncle Chaim. It's possible you remember me as a child. Maybe you've forgotten. It binds us, our old Shtetl, Sierpc, with our bygone youth and the Jewish life that we left there. From our Sierpc with 6,000 Jews there remains a few tens who can be counted on one's fingers all of them, our closest and best all our friends have perished at the hands of the murderous bands from Deuchtland *(Germany)*. What is left is only a memory and a tear in one's heart. Remember us for a blessing - all our dearest.

I received your address from Wolf Bida and soon I will be in communication with you, thereby also will we be holding the thread of our dearest and nearest.

My life history in the great war I will not tell you in this letter. It is too long. It could be that in America, if I will arrive, we will talk this through and relate about the great Jewish tragedy. My story is an ordeal of suffering and pain from a survivor Jew. I find myself in Germany already 8 months. I was also in our Sierpc for a few months. It was difficult to endure that. All the houses are still standing but without Jews. It appears sorrowful - there are no Jews with their payos, nor our youth who used to promenade in the market and on Plodiker St. There is a general fright for only the thought that here lived your acquaintances and near ones and a fear overcomes you - the cemetery plowed under, the trees chopped down, there is no longer a remainder. One can no longer remain there *(in Sierpc);* I have left everything and came over here. I live here in a UNRRA camp. I have also hopes to come to America, but it has now become more difficult. It is possible that you can have some influence in the consulate of the relief committee; with this, you can help me. My papers are already with the consulate, but I still have no visa. My papers were sent to me by my cousin, his address: A. Wolman,[137] 2453-64 St, Brooklyn, NY. I really would like to come to America; there is no future for life here. Also here is my younger brother Moshe and his wife, who just arrived from Russia. My parents were saved and are now in Poland. I send very hearty regards to you and your wife and family. I wish you all the best.

Your good acquaintance,

Shayah Lelonek

P.S. In return, you can answer to the address on the envelope. It is Moshe Aharon Neubach from Drobin, you surely know him.

Your acquaintance,

Shayah

---

[137] Pesa Kadecki's sister, Rachel married Moshe Hersch Wolman, their oldest son was Abram Wolman.

Undated note:

About me, there is no news. I am healthy; also my dear parents, sisters, and brothers. I can share with you that my sister Manya is marrying Yitzchak Hutnik from Sierpc. The wedding is taking place the 18th of February, 1947 in Lampertheim. It should be a mazeldik[138] time. I continue to think about coming to America. I have already done quite a bit in this regard, but it is going with great difficulty. Certainly by now, Baruch Niemoff has arrived; he is Ita Niemoff's son. He has come to Wolf Bida.

March 16, 1947

Dear and honored Sierpcer friends!

At first and in the beginning of my letter, I express my hearty thanks to our relief committee from our Sierpcer townsfolk for the memorial book that I have received today. It is perhaps the only memory, the only remnant from our former hometown with our former life history from a civil society that existed until the year 1941 and is no longer. The tears are stuck in one's throat, the heart breaks from hurt, reading the names of our most loved, dear, and closest holy ones, kedoshim, who have perished in such a beastly manner at the hands of Hitler's bandits. We bow our heads to the fallen and murdered - our sisters and brothers!!! To eternal memory!

I have in this time written a few letters to Mordechai Reshotko and clarified for him piecemeal about me and also our family. We are here among the singular families that were by some miracle saved from the heavy folk tragedy. It is not so simple or obvious to maintain a family whole. One can't perhaps write out, and I hope that when I have the

---

[138] Opportune time governed by fate/astrological signs.

opportunity when I am together with you in America, will we be able to discuss and clarify things which are not until today still not clear. I, myself, Shayah Lelonek, have endured a history of suffering and pain on the battlefield until the German captivity in camps. Fate wanted me to remain alive and be able to tell all in freedom. Maybe there are already with you Sierpcer people who came after the war and they will explain to you, more or less, a chapter of Jewish life in the years 1939-1945.

I can with deep, difficulty, share with you an episode that was related to me by survivors about the lives and demise of my uncle Shlomo Lelonek's children. My uncle's children were away to Warsaw in 1939. There they lived a difficult war life. Their son-in-law *(Shlomo Lelonek's son in law)* Shaul Widorowitz, born in Ratzonz, helped them with everything after the liquidation in the year 1943 of the Warsaw ghetto. Shaul Widorowitz hid the entire family in a bunker. In the year 1944, they were captured through Poles and were turned over to the German Gestapo. Manya Lelonek, Boruch Lelonek, and the young Chaim were shot immediately, and Rochel Widorowitz with her daughter, a six-year-old girl, and her husband, Shaul Widorowitz were brought to "Powiac," that is a Warsaw prison. From there, Rochel and her young daughter on one early morning were terminated and Shaul Widorowitz went away from the prison with a group of friends and hid themselves in a bunker. After great suffering and tortures, a frightful endurance of hunger and thirst, they managed to remain alive until the great day of liberation of Warsaw by the "Red Army." They had lived until liberation in a cellar in a bombed-out house on a street where there was no longer any living human presence. Exhausted from the great tragedy and suffering, Shaul Widorowitz drags himself in the beginning of February 1945 to Sierpc. He was the first Jew to return to Sierpc. He went to his home in Dales St. by the baker Gradzicki and wanted to search there for anything *(remaining)* of his possessions. In the evening, ostensible military men from the security service entered the house and demanded that he establish his identity and took him away. And thus went away from that moment and he in a secretive manner perished through the murderous Polish hands. I, coming to Sierpc from Germany in June 1945 tried everything to find some scent of his body, but all was without success.

I have a request for you - that you remain in constant contact with me and write me about everything. I, from my side, will always send you letters. I greet you very heartily my Sierpcer friends and wish you great success in life. Special regards to our m'chutan[139] Mordechai Reshotko and his family, also to my neighbor Golda Goldman and all the other Sierpcer townsfolk.

From your friend,

Shayah Lelonek

---

[139] Relatives through marriage.

MOSHE'S LETTERS

Moshe Lelonek, 25 years old in 1947, written in Yiddish.

March 31, 1947

To the friend Mordechai Reshotko,

It will be winter when you receive this letter. Oh, how I wish that we could meet in person. I declare that I am the son of Yitzchak Mayer Lelonek of Sierpc. I am today in Lampertheim, living in one house with my parents, with my wife and my 2-year-old daughter. You imagine for yourself how life is here. We returned to the camp *(Lampertheim displaced persons camp)* in Germany. Everyone lives with whomever he has. This doesn't hit upon our physical and moral situation. I don't even write one request in response to your aid within the limits of what is possible for you. I feel that you have not forgotten me, even though I am apart from you. I am able to tell you that the Sierpcers received the packages that you sent. I received the package that was sent to me by my brother, Shayah. I thank you very much for your assistance. I remember that you agreed to accept my request.

Please send me regards to my uncle, Wolf *(Kadetsky)* and his family,

Moshe[140] and his family, to my cousin, Abraham Kadetsky, to my colleagues and the landsmanshaft.

Your friend,

Moshe Lelonek

June 8, 1947

Dear Sierpcer Relief Committee,

I have written to you a while ago, and a lot of time has passed and I have not yet heard back from you. I think it is possible that my letter did not get to you, and it is upon me to tell you whom I am. I am the son of Yitzchak Mayer Lelonek from Sierpc. I live in Lampertheim with my wife and 2-year-old daughter. Until a short time ago I did not know there was a Relief Committee in America. But the people of Sierpc who live here say that they received help from you. Our situation, you for sure know. I, myself, work, but can you add to my earnings in order that I can reduce the conditions of my existence. Specifically, since I have with me a small daughter. If you can, please pass on the message of Shalom to the sons of Sierpc and good friend, Baruch Niemoff, who lived with us a certain time here together. I turn to you with a request. Here in Lampertheim, a certain amount of fellow countrymen received help from you. We have seen the assistance but we have not merited to derive benefit from it. Therefore, I hope, that it is enough what I have said above, that you will do what you are able to do on our behalf. First and foremost, I request that you guard the connection of the letter between us. I await your speedy response. The wife and daughter pass along well wishes to all the countrymen.

---

[140] Likely a reference to uncle Moshe Wolman and his son Abe Wolman. Abe Wolman was in contact with Charlie. Pesa Kadecki's sister, Rachel married Moshe Hersch Wolman, their oldest son was Abe Wolman.

From me,

Moshe Lelonek

September 30, 1947

Summary:

Honored Sierpcer Relief Committee,

Moshe Lelonek is married and has a 2-year-old daughter for whom he asks the relief committee to send warm clothes (wool) and shoes because he can't get those items in the displaced persons camp and the winter is already there, they feel the cold in their bones. He works at the displaced persons camp school and asks the relief committee to send him a Hebrew-Yiddish-Hebrew dictionary. He says they came to the displaced persons camp with the understanding that it was a temporary arrangement, but they have already started their second year there and they see no light at the end of the tunnel as the situation, in all its aspects, gets worse every day.

From me,

Moshe Lelonek

Underneath is the decision taken by the committee: to send him a parcel with clothes for the child and the dictionary he asked for.

October 10, 1947

Dear esteemed Sierpc fellow-townsfolk,

As I don't want to lose touch with you, I'm taking a little time to write you a few words. We are all well, even though life is very hard. After all, we carry on. A few days ago, I received a package from you. We thank you very much for your assistance to us, as well as for not forgetting us. It goes without saying that the package will be very useful to us because this is our only help. I've written to you several times, but have received no answer from you. I don't know why this is the case, and it is very surprising, but maybe it's not your fault. In our life now and the situation we find ourselves in, even a few words from good friends are encouraging. We hope that we will soon get to a permanent place, and all our troubles will be ended. Though you don't know them, my family, wife, and child send their regards to you. We send heartfelt greetings to all the Sierpc compatriots.

From me,

Moshe Lelonek

YITZCHAK HUTNIK'S LETTERS

Yitzchak Hutnik, 30 years old in 1917, written in Yiddish.

August 2, 1947, Lampertheim

Honored Friends of the Sierpcer landsman committee!!

Having not yet received a letter dealing with the Sierpcer relief, I would like to describe to you my personal autobiography, and my membership in the Sierpcer landsmanshaft. I am Yitzchak Hutnik from Sierpc. I lived with my parents in the Sierpc Mikvah Street. Our neighbors were the R' Yossel Zikhel family who are now in America. My mother is Rochel-Leah Hutnik, David Magid's daughter. I and my younger brother, Yechiel Hutnik, alone survived. From the rest of the family, we alone survived.

I recently married Yitzchak Mayer Lelonek's daughter, Manya who is also from Sierpc.

From all the donor packages and money that you have sent through Germany, you have not yet shown an interest in us.

And maybe you deny something to buy for the first time. I do not hear from you but you reply to all other the Sierpcer. It seems that because I'm poor, they're ashamed of me.

I think that the whole thing is clear to you and that you will strive to fix the matter. I await your answer impatiently. My wife and I send you our heartfelt regards.

We wish you a lucky and joyful year.

From Yitzchak Hutnik and wife.

October 29, 1947, Lampertheim

Honored gentlemen Mordechai Reshotko,

We received your letter for which we thank you very much.

It seems that you have an interest in our landsmanshaft and in our old home. It's possible that my previous letter upset you a little. But you should understand the feeling of a minority are like us. But as it turns out, it was only a misunderstanding, and neither our friends nor I are to blame. I think that in the future everything will be all right and we will stay in close contact with our relief. I would like to explain the mistake to you but even better to meet you.

I have already written to you who I am but I'll do it again. My parents are the Hutniks of Sierpc, on Mikvah Street, next to the old ritual slaughterer R' Yossel Zikhel. My parent's nickname was "Magid." I, Yitzchak Hutnik, and my brother Yechiel Hutnik are the only ones of our whole family who remained alive. I live in Lampertheim at the given address, at my in-laws' place. My brother Yechiel Hutnik is still single and lives with my cousin Meir Hutnik's place in Wetslar. He is not from Sierpc; he is from......(missing rest of letter.)

January 17, 1948, Lampertheim

Honored Sierpcer friends from Relief,

We are letting you know that the package that you sent we received in order. We thank you for not forgetting us. Nothing is of more importance. We know the whole relief and we are hoping to stay in further contact with you.

From,

Yitzchak and Motel Hutnik.

A special regards from our parents, Yitzchak Mayer and Pesa Lelonek and family

GENIA'S LETTERS

Genia Lelonek; 16 years old; written in Polish.

June 30, 1947, Lampertheim,

Hello Bolek,

While staying at my cousins, I received your greetings for which I am very thankful. I am still living in Bad Wörishofen. I am no longer in a sanatorium or in a kibbutz. I currently live in a lager,[141] it is a small camp, which is actually a house with 50 persons living in it. Just imagine - I am now totally self-reliant. I am not sure if I can manage but I have tried. As you know, things are now getting worse. I would like to be on some road, as now I am neither on a land nor on water. Life is very tough - an ongoing battle. It is really bad when you have no strengths to fight this battle. Therefore, I live in hope and believe that tomorrow will be better, but would I live long enough? I have asked the question but have not received the answer. How are you? Have you settled in? How are you spending your time? Do you mind me asking? You haven't responded to my questions so I will ask again. What are your plans for future? Nothing new is happening here. What is your

---

[141] A camp

impression of America? I don't think you need to ration calories in America like we do here. I would like to finish my letter by sending you my kind regards and best wishes for all your endeavors.

I remain yours truly,

Genia

PS: Please do not forget about me and write to me. Best regards to everyone.

Genia

PS: You can pass my best regards to the Sierpc Committee. I hope they won't forget about me - I am part of Sierpc's community.

June 30, 1947, Lampertheim

Dear Mrs. Goldman

While staying at my cousins in Lampertheim, I received a letter from Mr. Sina who is enquiring about Dadek Klajman. I would like to advise you that I have not met any Dadek. There must have been some misunderstanding between those boys as I have seen Moshe Goldman, son of Shifra Faiga Goldman, née Flatau. I would like to take this opportunity to mention a few words about myself. You probably know who I am. I am Genia Lelonek, daughter of Yitzchak Lelonek, born in Sierpc. I would like to ask the Sierpc Committee not to forget about me as, so far, I have not received any assistance. I have met a number of other people from Sierpc who were surprised that that I have not taken advantage despite the fact that I am almost the youngest survivor from Sierpc. If it is possible, I would like to ask for a Yizkor book.

Warm regards to all fellow citizens of Sierpc.

Kind regards,

Genia Lelonek

My address:

Genia Lelonek, Bad Wörishofen 136, Lindenallestr 9e, Hotel Luiers, US Zone (Obbayern) Germany

PS: You can pass my best regards to the Sierpc Committee. I hope they won't forget about me - I am part of Sierpc's community.

(Note written by the Sierpc Relief Committee:)

February - June

2 boxes sent by Care 2/10; 6/10

PART VI

NECROLOGY

CHAPTER 20:
LELONEK FAMILY'S HOLOCAUST NECROLOGY

Family name(s)	First name(s)	Dates	Father's name	Mother's name	Name of spouse	Relationship to Charlie
LELONEK	Yitzchak		Chaim	Baila	Billa	1st cousin 1 removed
LELONEK	Ila		Josef	Dwojra Typris	Yitzchak	1st cousin 1 removed
LELONEK	Chana Dvora		Yitzchak	Billa		2nd cousin
LELONEK	Efrayim Yossel		Yitzchak	Billa		2nd cousin
LELONEK	Sarah Mania	7/7/15-2/19/43	Yitzchak	Billa		2nd cousin
LELONEK	Jacob		Yitzchak	Billa		2nd cousin
LELONEK	Chaim		Yitchak	Billa		2nd cousin
LELONEK	Chaya		Yitzchak	Billa		2nd cousin
LELONEK	Shlomo Zalman	1885-	Abraham	Miriam	Miriam	Uncle
LELONEK	Miriam				Shlomo Zalman	Aunt
LELONEK	Mendel	1912-	Shlomo Zalman	Miriam		1st cousin
LELONEK	Baruch	1915-	Shlomo Zalman	Miriam		1st cousin

WIDOROWITZ	Rachel	1916-	Shlomo	Miriam		1st cousin
WIDOROWITZ	Shaul					
LELONEK	Mania Miatal	1920-	Shlomo Zalman	Miriam		1st cousin
LELONEK	Chaim	4/7/23-1/15/43	Shlomo Zalman	Miriam		1st cousin
LELONEK	Chaim	1917-1940	Icek Majer	Pesa		Brother
LELONEK	Miriam		Salomon	Chana Kominski	Chaim	Aunt
LELONEK	Esther				Zalmen	1st cousin
LELONEK	Zalman		Chaim	Miriam Czarna	Esther	1st cousin
LELONEK	Bluma		Zalman	Ester Rosenfeld		1st cousin
LELONEK	Gitel		Chaim	Miriam Czarna		1st cousin
PLOTNIARZ	Sara Bracha		Abraham Lelonek	Miriam		Aunt
KADECKI	Yechezkel	1875	Israel	Rosa Rakow	Rivkah	Uncle
KADECKI	Rivkah	1880-1941	Uziel Moshe	Zelda	Yechezkel	Aunt
CZARNY	Bina				Shmuel	1st cousin
CZARNY	Shmuel		Yitzchak	Rivka	Bina	1st cousin

CZARNY	Avraham		Shmuel	Bina		1st cousin 1 removed
CZARNY	Yitzchak		Shmuel	Bina		1st cousin 1 removed
KADECKI	Gitel Leah		Yechezkel	Rivkah		1st cousin
KADECKI	Moshe	3/30/09- 1/22/43	Yechezkel	Rivkah	Sheine Rivkah	1st cousin
KADECKI	Sheine Rivkah	1908-	Avraham	Mindel	Moshe	1st cousin

GLOSSARY

Adonoy, hu haElohim: Hebrew. Lit. "The Master, only He is G-d." This is the last line of the ending prayer of Yom Kippur, the Neilah (closing) Service. The Jewish people at the end of the service declare G-d's sovereignty seven times. The seven pronunciations symbolize the seven levels of heaven through which God ascends and returns after the Yom Kippur service.

Aliyot: Hebrew. Spiritual elevations of the soul in the world to come.

Chazzan: Hebrew. Prayer leader.

Chuppah: Hebrew. Jewish wedding canopy.

Gemilut Chasadim: Hebrew. Lit. Loving kindness. A community charity organization.

HaNoar HaTzioni: Hebrew. Lit. The Young Zionists.

HaShomer HaTzair: Hebrew. Lit. The Youth Guard.

Kaddish: Hebrew. Memorial prayer.

Kedoshim: Hebrew. Lit. Holy ones. Used in reference to people that died in the name of G-d.

Kehilat Sierpc; Sefer Zikaron: Hebrew. Lit. Community of Sierpc Memorial Book.

Kosher: Hebrew. Jewish dietary laws.

Lager: German. Lit. A camp.

Landsmanshaft: Yiddish. A fraternal organization made up of Jewish immigrants from the same region.

M'chutan: Hebrew. Relatives through marriage.

Mazeldik: Yiddish. Opportune time governed by fate/astrological signs.

Minyan: Hebrew. Gathering of ten men and a quorum for Jewish public prayer.

Mussaf: Hebrew. An added prayer service for the Sabbath, new month and holidays.

Neshamah: Hebrew. Soul.

Olam haba: Hebrew. Lit. The world to come.

Passover: Holiday celebrating emancipation and the Exodus from Egypt.

Payos: Hebrew. Sideburns or side locks.

Purim: Hebrew. Holiday commemorate the story of Esther.

Rosh HaShanah: Hebrew. Holiday celebrating Jewish New Year.

Schnell: German. Lit. Quick.

Shivah: Hebrew. Jewish mourning period for seven days after the burial of the deceased.

Shmatas: Yiddish. Rags.

Shochet: Hebrew. Kosher butcher.

Shofar: Hebrew. Ram's horn fashioned into a wind instrument, sounded one hundred times each of the two days of Rosh HaShanah.

Simchat Torah: Hebrew. The holiday following Sukkot, celebrating the completion of the yearly cycle of reading the Torah, bible.

Sukkah: Hebrew. The huts that Jews dwell in during the holiday of Sukkot. The sukkahs commemorate the way the Jews lived in the desert after the Exodus from Egypt and symbolize that people are reliant on G-d's beneficence.

Sukkot: Hebrew. The holiday commemorating the ways Jews lived after the Exodus from Egypt, in huts for forty years in the desert before entering the Land of Israel.

Tallis: Hebrew. Four cornered prayer shawl with strings tied around the corners worn during the prayer service.

Tefillin: Hebrew. Phylacteries are two small black boxes containing specific biblical texts written on parchment. Using long black painted leather straps, one box is wound around the non-dominant arm with the box facing the heart and the other box wound around the head during the daily morning prayer services. They symbolize serving G-d with one's heart and mind.

Tishah B'Av: Hebrew. 9th of the Hebrew month of Av, memorializing the destruction of the temples in Jerusalem. Many other Jewish community tragedies are memorialized as well.

Yahrzeit: Yiddish. Death anniversary according the Jewish lunar calendar.

Yiddisha gas: Yiddish. Lit. Jewish section.

Yizkor book: Memorial books were written by survivors to preserve the memory of their towns and the people murdered in the Holocaust.

Yizkor gatherings: Hebrew. Communities came together on a day significant to their European town to memorialize the victims and deceased survivors.

Yom Kippur: Hebrew. Day of atonement spent fasting and praying in the synagogue after reflecting and repenting.

Zaml Book Fun Sierpcer Shairit HaChurban: Yiddish. Lit. The Complete Book of the Sierpcer People Left Over From the Destruction.

Zionist: The philosophical desire of the Jewish people to return to the Land of Israel.

Gary Lelonek is a Child and Adolescent Emergency Department Psychiatrist in New York City where he lives with his wife and kids. He has studied the impact of knowledge of family history on the development of resilience in children.

Made in the USA
Lexington, KY
23 July 2016